William Shakespeare's

A Midsummer Night's Dream

Includes Study Guide, Historical Context, Biography, and Character Index

BookCaps™ Study Guides

www.bookcaps.com

Cover Image © Algol - Fotolia.com

Table of Contents

Lesson Plans

Introduction

-
- "A Midsummer Night's Dream" is different from anything else Shakespeare ever wrote. He pulls from his education (Greek Mythology) and his wild imagination to create this one of a kind play. He even pulls from old English lore, utilizing characters from all areas, even using characters from other plays being put on during the same time period. This is a comedy of errors, a story of love, and a story of constant mishaps and misunderstandings, and the struggles of trying to "fix:" what you broke by mistake. It was made into a movie in 1999, with a cast including Kevin Kline and Michelle Pfeiffer.

-
- Throughout these lessons, students will learn the various lessons Shakespeare attempted to portray in his story of finding and keeping love.

-

Lesson Plan Format

-
-
- Shakespeare as a man, poet, and writer is significant. He was highly influenced by what was happening around him in Elizabethan England. During each session, students will read portions of the play, look at historical context for what was written, delve into the various controversies that surround William Shakespeare, and how these relate to his writings and the world today.

-
- Students should have a copy of "A Midsummer Night's Dream" to read and work with. If they do not, the following online resources can be used to read the text. Also, encompassed here are books and online resources the teacher can use in presenting the lessons:

-
- **Books:**
-
- Pennington, Michael. *A Midsummer Night's Dream: A User's Guide*. London: Nick Hern, 2005.

-
- Shakespeare, William. *A Midsummer Night's Dream*. Cambridge: University, 1936.

-
- Shurin, Aaron. *William Shakespeare's A Midsummer Night's Dream*. Woodbury, NY: Barron's Educational Series, 1985.

-
- **Websites:**
-
    - Shakespeare, William. "Midsummer Night's Dream: Entire Play." *Midsummer Night's*
- *Dream: Entire Play*. MIT, 1993. Web. 27 Sept. 2012. <http://shakespeare.mit.edu/midsummer/full.html>.

-

- Shakespeare, William. "A Midsummer Night's Dream :|: Open Source Shakespeare." *A Midsummer Night's Dream :|: Open Source Shakespeare*. Open Source, 2003. Web. 27 Sept. 2012. <http://www.opensourceshakespeare.org/views/plays/playmenu.php? WorkID=midsummer>.

-

Writer's Journal

-
- Writers have been using journals to keep track of daily activities, their thoughts, their inspirations, and their life questions for as long as there has been the written word. Journals can be used for free-writing or to facilitate classroom discussion. They can be a way for students to discover what they know and don't know about a subject. Journals are also perfect for students who may be too shy to speak their thoughts and opinions aloud.

-
- These journals will be used to answer specific writing prompts, complete class and homework assignments, including drawings and writings, and also for a way to communicate with their teacher any questions that may arise as they work through the lessons.

-

Standards

-
- **Common Core State Standards for ELA**

From NCTE (National Council of Teachers of English)

Common Core Standards – Literature Craft and Structure	Grade 9-12
Area 4	**Grade 9-10:** Determine the meaning of words and phrases as they are used in the text, including figurative and connotative meanings; analyze the cumulative impact of specific word choices on meaning and tone (e.g., how the language evokes a sense of time and place; how it sets a formal or informal tone). **Grade 11-12:** Determine the meaning of words and phrases as they are used in the text, including figurative and connotative meanings; analyze the impact of specific word choices on meaning and tone, including words with multiple meanings or language that is particularly fresh, engaging, or beautiful. (Include Shakespeare as well as other authors.)
Area 5	**Grade 9-10:** Analyze how an author's choices concerning how to structure a text, order events within it (e.g., parallel plots), and manipulate time (e.g., pacing, flashbacks) create such effects as mystery, tension, or surprise. **Grade 11-12:** Analyze how an author's choices concerning how to structure specific parts of a text (e.g., the choice of where to begin or end a story, the choice to provide a comedic or tragic resolution) contribute to its overall structure and meaning as well as its aesthetic impact.

Common Core Standards - Literature Key Ideas and Details	Grades 9 -12
Area 1	**Grade 9-10:** Cite strong and thorough textual evidence to support analysis of what the text says explicitly as well as inferences drawn from the text. **Grade 11-12:** Cite strong and thorough textual evidence to support analysis of what the text says explicitly as well as inferences drawn from the text, including determining where the text leaves matters uncertain
Area 2	**Grade 9-10:** Determine a theme or central idea of a text and analyze in detail its development over the course of the text, including how it emerges and is shaped and refined by specific details; provide an objective summary of the text. **Grade 11-12:** Determine two or more themes or central ideas of a text and analyze their development over the course of the text, including how they interact and build on one another to produce a complex account; provide an objective summary of the text.
Area 3	**Grade 9-10:** Analyze how complex characters (e.g., those with multiple or conflicting motivations) develop over the course of a text, interact with other characters, and advance the plot or develop the theme. **Grade 11-12:** Analyze the impact of the author's choices regarding how to develop and relate elements of a story or drama (e.g., where a story is set, how the action is ordered, how the characters are introduced and developed).

Common Core Standards – Literature Integration of Knowledge and Ideas	Grade: 9-12
Area 9	**Grade 9-10:** Analyze how an author draws on and transforms source material in a specific work (e.g., how Shakespeare treats a theme or topic from Ovid or the Bible or how a later author draws on a play by Shakespeare).

●

Common Core Standards – Writing Text Type and Purposes	Grade 9-12
Area 1	**Grade 9-12:** Write arguments to support claims in an analysis of substantive topics or texts, using valid reasoning and relevant and sufficient evidence.
Area 2	**Grade 9-12:** Write informative/explanatory texts to examine and convey complex ideas, concepts, and information clearly and accurately through the effective selection, organization, and analysis of content.
Area 3	**Grade 9-12:** Write narratives to develop real or imagined experiences or events using effective technique, well-chosen details, and well-structured event sequences.

Common Core Standards – Writing Production and Distribution of Writing	Grade 9-12
Area 4	**Grade 9-12:** Produce clear and coherent writing in which the development, organization, and style are appropriate to task, purpose, and audience. (Grade-specific expectations for writing types are defined in standards 1–3 above.)
Area 5	**Grade 9-12:** Develop and strengthen writing as needed by planning, revising, editing, rewriting, or trying a new approach, focusing on addressing what is most significant for a specific purpose and audience.
Area 6	**Grade 9-12:** Use technology, including the Internet, to produce, publish, and update individual or shared writing products, taking advantage of technology's capacity to link to other information and to display information flexibly and dynamically.

Common Core Standards – Writing Research to Build and present knowledge	Grade 9-12
Area 7	**Grade 9-12:** Conduct short as well as more sustained research projects to answer a question (including a self-generated question) or solve a problem; narrow or broaden the inquiry when appropriate; synthesize multiple sources on the subject, demonstrating understanding of the subject under investigation.
Area 8	**Grade 9-12:** Gather relevant information from multiple authoritative print and digital sources, using advanced searches effectively; assess the usefulness of each source in answering the research question; integrate information into the text selectively to maintain the flow of ideas, avoiding plagiarism and following a standard format for citation.
Area 9	**Grade 9-12:** Draw evidence from literary or informational texts to support analysis, reflection, and research.

Common Core Standards – Writing Range of Writing	Grade 9-12
Area 10	**Grade 9-12:** Write routinely over extended time frames (time for research, reflection, and revision) and shorter time frames (a single sitting or a day or two) for a range of tasks, purposes, and audiences.

Common Core Standards – Language Conventions of Standard English	Grade 9-12
Area 1	**Grade 9-10:** Demonstrate command of the conventions of standard English grammar and usage when writing or speaking. a. Use parallel structure. b. Use various types of phrases (noun, verb, adjectival, adverbial, participial, prepositional, absolute) and clauses (independent, dependent; noun, relative, adverbial) to convey specific meanings and add variety and interest to writing or presentations. **Grade 11-12:** Demonstrate command of the conventions of standard English grammar and usage when writing or speaking. a. Apply the understanding that usage is a matter of convention, can change over time, and is sometimes contested. b. Resolve issues of complex or contested usage, consulting references (e.g., *Merriam-Webster's Dictionary of English Usage, Garner's Modern American Usage*) as needed.
Area 2	**Grade 9-12:** Demonstrate command of the conventions of standard English capitalization, punctuation, and spelling when writing

Common Core Standards – Language Knowledge of Language	Grade 9-12
Area 3	**Grade 9-12:** Apply knowledge of language to understand how language functions in different contexts, to make effective choices for meaning or style, and to comprehend more fully when reading or listening.

Common Core Standards – Language Vocabulary Acquisition and Use	Grade 9-12
Area 4	**Grade 9-12:** Determine or clarify the meaning of unknown and multiple-meaning words and phrases based, choosing flexibly from a range of strategies.
Area 5	**Grade 9-12:** Demonstrate understanding of figurative language, word relationships, and nuances in word meanings.

- Retrieved from: **http://www.ncte.org/standards**
- Grade 9-12 Common Core Standards – ELA: **http://www.corestandards.org/assets/CCSSI_ELA%20Standards.pdf**
-
  - *Use your state and district standards to align these common core*
    - *standards with your lesson plans.*
-
-

Sample Rubrics

-
- General Rubrics:
- **http://rubistar.4teachers.org/**
- **http://www.rcampus.com/indexrubric.cfm**
- **http://www.teach-nology.com/web_tools/rubrics/**

-
  - Writing Rubrics
- **http://www.rubrics4teachers.com/writing.php**
- **http://www.teach-nology.com/web_tools/rubrics/writing/**
  -
  - Graphic Organizers
- **http://www.eduplace.com/graphicorganizer/**
- **http://www.educationoasis.com/curriculum/graphic_orga nizers.htm**
- **http://www.teachervision.fen.com/graphic-organizers/printable/6293.html**
  -
  - Resources Needed
- Dictionary
- Thesaurus
- Internet Access
- Writing Journal
- Pens/Pencils
- PosterBoard
- Markers/Crayons/Colored Pencils
- Glue/Adhesive

-
-

Sample Schedule

-
- **Day/Session 1**
-
- Biography/Historical Context
-
- **Day/Session 2**
-
- Narrative/Structure/POV of "A Midsummer's Night Dream"
-
- **Day/Session 3**
-
- Characters and Character Development
-
- **Day/Session 4**
-
- Themes/Symbols/Figurative Language
-
- **Day/Session 5**
-
- What Makes it a Great Book?
-

Day One: Shakespeare Biography & Historical Context

-
-

Objective

-
- Students will gain a better understanding of "A Midsummer Night's Dream" if they understand the life of William Shakespeare and the era he grew up in. They will be able to see and understand how history affected Shakespeare's writing and the controversy surrounding his life and works. Students will be able to demonstrate their knowledge and understanding of Elizabethan England as well as how Shakespeare's influence still reaches us today.

-
- For today students should read Act I of "A Midsummer Night's Dream".

-

Discussion Questions/Writing Journal Responses

-
1. (Prewrite) What do you know about "A Midsummer Night's Dream"? When you hear the name William Shakespeare, what comes to mind? For this assignment just write everything you know (or think you know) about Shakespeare and "A Midsummer Night's Dream". Also, write down any questions you may have.

-
2. Thinking about what you've learned about William Shakespeare: his upbringing, his writings, his education, etc., what do you think happened during those ten "lost" years?

3. In the Elizabethan era, plays were not considered good literature or even praiseworthy reading material. Based on what you've learned about history during this time, why do you think that is?

-

4. Starting with Shakespeare's birth what where the principal events of his life, and how do you think they influenced his writings?

-

5. *The Globe*. What is the significance of it? When did it come into play? How does it compare to theatres today? Include an illustration with your response, making sure it is labeled properly.

-

6. Given the discussion on blank verse and iambic pentameter, find examples of this in "A Midsummer Night's Dream". How did Shakespeare's writing style change written language as it was known during Elizabethan England? Give some examples for comparison.

7. When was "A Midsummer Night's Dream" first written; when and where was it first performed; and who were the performers?

-

8. What was Shakespeare's influence in writing this play? Remember, everything Shakespeare did has a purpose, what was the point of this?

9. Take the main characters you've met so far in the play and write down what you think about them. Do you like them? What part do you believe they will play in the remainder of the story? Give examples of what you think – use quotes from the play.

10. Some say that Shakespeare wasn't really Shakespeare. Some way he stole all these writings and then published them under his name. Others believe it was multiple people working together and using this assumed name. Still others believe it was a nobleman who didn't want his friends and family to know he was writing such crass material. What do you think and why? Find proof to back up your thoughts.

Homework Assignments

- <u>Links</u>
-
- Globe Theatre History
- **http://www.william-shakespeare.info/william-shakespeare-globe-theatre.htm**
- BBC Video History of the Globe
- **http://www.bbc.co.uk/learningzone/clips/shakespeare-and-the-globe-theatre/3342.html**
- **Globe Theatre Pictures**
- Elizabethan England
- **http://www.bardweb.net/england.html**

1. **Foreshadowing Essay**: You've read the Act I of the play. There is foreshadowing in Act I Scene 1 which gives us hints of what is to come. What is this incident and what do you think it foretells? What does this tell us about each character so far in the play? Give examples to back up your thoughts.

2. **Design Time**: Design your own Globe Theatre! You can use whatever materials you would like to create your 3D replica of Shakespeare's Globe Theatre. Each section must be labeled correctly. Along with your replica, please provide a description of each section: names, what they were used for, who used them, and any other facts you may have found fascinating (will be 1-2 pages in length).

3. **Biography**: Get to know Queen Elizabeth – the woman the Elizabethan Age was named after. Write a 3-4 page biography on the woman who influenced a nation. This will NOT just be a recap of her life – how did her decisions affect England during her reign and for years after? Make sure to give your insights and back up what you state. Use MLA formatting throughout.

4. **Timeline**: Create a timeline of historically significant events during Elizabethan England, carefully adding in Shakespeare's own timeline. Make sure you complete it in two different colors so that overlaps and patterns can emerge. Once you've completed it, look for patterns and write a 1-2 page essay on what you see – how did they affect one another?

5. **Gaming**: Take the facts you have learned about Shakespeare and Elizabethan England and create a board game. You must have at least 20 questions about each (so 40 total) – more is acceptable, but not less. Your game must have a clear beginning, purpose, path (how it's played/directions) and a clear way to win/end. You can create something ordinary like SORRY© or something as complex as Monopoly or Trivial Pursuit. You will need pictures, poster board (or cardboard), markers, glue, crayons, etc. Don't forget to write out the directions.

6. **Art Fair:** This was a terrific time of writing, painting, and history. Find pictures of the art that speaks to you. Create a poster and/or collage of what you like. You must have at least 10 images. For each image, you will write 1-2 paragraphs (4-6 sentences each paragraph) about why you chose that piece.

   •

Day 2: Narrative, Structure, and Point of View

-

Objective

-
- In today's lesson/session students will learn about narratives, how they are structured, point of view, and how each relates to "A Midsummer Night's Dream". Each plays a strong role in how Shakespeare shares the point of his play. Journals will be used to facilitate class discussion; homework will further critical thinking skills, and application skills as well as helping students learn to see Shakespeare's relevance today.

-
- According to the Merriam Webster Dictionary, a narrative is a "story, or a representation in art of an event or story". Structure is "the action of building or something that is arranged in a definite pattern of organization". Lastly, point of view is "the position from which something is considered or evaluated".

-
- Students are expected to read Act II of the play for this section.

-

Discussion Questions/Writing Journal Responses

-
1. What is the difference between reading this play and reading other works you've come across? Think of at least 3 things and describe them. Use your notes and books if need be. Also, if you have any questions about these differences, write them down, as well.

-
2. Thinking about narratives and how they tell a story, but that they can also represent something else in order to tell about an event, what do you believe is the purpose behind Shakespeare's "A Midsummer Night's Dream"? Use

information you've learned about Shakespeare, Elizabethan England, and what you have read thus far.

•

3. The literal meaning behind structure is building. Structure for literary works also refers to how it was built and the purpose of putting the written word together the way the author did. It implies a deliberate set up of each word and line in the play. What is your opinion about this? Did Shakespeare write deliberately?

•

4. Whose point of view is "A Midsummer Night's Dream" written? Why is this relevant? What would it be like if someone else "told" the story?

•

5. It's time to look at the remaining characters. At this point, you've "met" all the main characters in the play. What do you think about those you've just met? Have any of your opinions of other characters changed? Don't forget to explain your answers and give examples.

•

6. Here, some of the most famous quotes from Act I and Act II of the play:

    a. "The course of true love never did run smooth". Quote (Act I, Scene I)

    b. "Love looks, not with the eyes, but with the mind, and, therefore, is winged Cupid painted blind". Quote (Act I, Scene I)

    c. That would hang us, every mother's son. (Quote. Act I, Scene II)

    d. I'll put a girdle round about the earth In forty minutes. (Quote Act II, Scene I)

    e. My heart is true as steel. (Quote. Act II, Scene I)

    f. I know a bank where the wild thyme blows, Where oxlips and the nodding violet grows, Quite overcanopied with luscious woodbine,

With sweet musk-roses and with eglantine.
(Quote Act II, Scene I)
- What do each of these quotes mean?
-
7. How did Theseus make Hippolyta fall in love with him? Is it true love? The theme of love will come up throughout the play and what people will do for it. What else do Theseus and Hippolyta stand for in the play?
   -
   -

Homework Assignments

-
- <u>Links</u>
- Shakespeare and Narrative – to offer example
- **http://www.ashgate.com/pdf/samplepages/narrating_the_visual_in_shakespeare_intro.pdf**
- Play Structure – Example from Hamlet
- **http://www.folger.edu/documents/lesson3-handout1.pdf**
- Point of View Breakdown
- **http://staff.fcps.net/tcarr/shortstory/pointofview.htm**
- Elizabethan Clothing
- **http://www.elizabethan-era.org.uk/elizabethan-clothing.htm**
- Elizabethan Masks
- **http://www.elizabethan-era.org.uk/elizabethan-masques.htm**
  -
  -

1. **Family Tree:** Using a poster (or your computer), create a family tree for both, for our main families. Make sure each person is labeled and shows their relationship to others. Include servants (of importance), as well.
   -
2. **Mini-Autobiography**: Think about your life for a moment. Now, think about the lives of Hermia, Demetrius, Titania, and the other main characters. Are there any similarities?

I'm sure there are differences. Write a compare and contrast essay (2 pages) looking at your life and comparing it with two of theirs.

3. **Interview**: Interview Puck. He seems to have his hands in everything. Think of at least 10 open-ended questions (no simple yes or no answers) that you would like to ask him. Write what you think their response would be based on what you've read in Act I and Act II.

4. **In Your Own Words:** Rewrite Act II Scene I or Scene II into whatever time period you choose. You can use accents, dialect, choose an era (20s, 50s, western, etc.) – the trick is to stay consistent and have fun with it.

5. **Wedding**: Since this is play about couples wanting to get married, design a wedding that you think the characters would like. Choose one of the couples and design their wedding and reception including food, clothes, music, etc. It will be set during the time period of the play.

●

Day 3: Characters and Character Development

-

Objective

-
- Without the characters, there would be no play. How do the characters change throughout the play? Do they change? These are the types of discussions to have with students during this lesson/session. Students will learn how character development moves a story along; how characters interact with each other, effecting the story; and how these character relationships parallel what students are living today (how they can be translated to today's world).

-
- Students are expected to read through Act III of the play.
-

Discussion Questions/Writing Journal Responses

-
1. Based on what other characters say about each other in Acts I – III how do we know who actually loves who? Make sure to use concrete examples from the play.

-
2. Puck uses a potion to make people fall in love literally at first sight. Do you think this can ever be real? What other explanation (or emotion) could someone be feeling?

3. Even before the potion is given, there are some issues about obeying ones parents/guardians and the consequences if they are disobeyed. What are the consequences? Do you believe this is fair? Why or why not?

4. What do you think was the most significant speech (or set of lines) in Act III of the play? Who says them, what do they mean, and why do you believe these lines are crucial to the play?

5. Helena and Hermia are each self-conscience about something. What is it, how does it affect the play, and is this any different from what teenagers go through today (or how they feel sometimes)?

6. In "A Midsummer Night's Dream," Puck is considered, by many, to be the most prominent character. Why do you think that is and do you agree or disagree with that statement?

7. Out of two pairs of lovers, Helena is the one we hear from the most; she forgives Demetrius even before she knows he loves Hermia because of a potion. Is this love or foolishness? Explain your answer.

8. Thinking of what you know so far about the play, how would you describe the character, Bottom? Be specific and give examples. Do you think he will change?

-
-

Homework Assignments

-
  - Links
- Shakespeare Character List
- **http://www.shakespeare-online.com/plays/characters/charactermain.html**
- 10 Best Shakespearean Characters
- **http://www.guardian.co.uk/culture/gallery/2012/mar/25/ten-best-shakespeare-characters-pictures#/?picture=387763692&index=0**
- Excerpt – Video
- **http://www.pbs.org/shakespeare/works/work135.html**
-
  -
1. **Editorial**: Start by reading your local and national newspapers for a few days. What types of topics do they

discuss in their editorials? Your job is to write an editorial on the following characters: Puck, Oberon, Titania, Hermia, Helena, Lysander, and Demtrious. Each editorial will be about 1 page in length.

-

2. **Timeline**: Start a timeline of events up until this point. You will finish it at the end of Act V. Take the crucial events: meetings, parties, love proclamations, etc. and place create a timeline. On the back of your poster, write a short summary (2-3 sentences) of why each event is noteworthy.

3. **Memoir**: Choose Demetrious or Lysander and write a short memoir, making sure to refer to the other main characters and how they make you feel. Speak from their point of view and in the way they would talk about their friends and enemies.

4. **Compare/Contrast**: Think about what you know about the families thus far. Create a Venn diagram detailing the similarities and differences. Keep it so you can add to it through the rest of the reading of the play.

5. **Costumes**: Knowing what you know about each character and Elizabethan England, design costumes for Puck, Hermia, Helena, and Titania. How would you update them for today? Make sure you label your drawings.

-

Day 4: Themes/Symbols/Figurative Language

-

Objective

-
- In this lesson/session students will review the themes, symbols, and figurative language happening throughout the play. Each of these plays a significant role in moving the play forward, character development, and overall understanding of the play. Shakespeare is brilliant at weaving themes and symbols into his works in a way that appeals to the masses and transcends time, making him relevant even today.

-
- **Symbols** are, "something used for or regarded as representing something else; a material object representing something, often something immaterial; emblem, token, or sign," per **www.dictionary.com**.

-
- **Themes**, according to **www.dictionary.com**, are a unifying or dominant idea, motif, etc.

-

Figurative Language is "language that contains or uses figures of speech, especially metaphors" and similes. This definition can also be found at **www.dictionary.com**.

-
- Students should read through Act IV for today's lesson.
-

Discussion Questions/Writing Journal Responses

-
1. There are three main symbols used in the play; write 1-2 paragraphs (4-7 sentences each) about what the symbols mean and how they are used in "A Midsummer Night's Dream". Can these symbols be found in literature today? Give examples.

-

2. What is the overarching theme to "A Midsummer Night's Dream"? It effects everything and everyone in the play; give examples, and also give examples from contemporary literature of each theme, as well.

3. Metaphors, similes, hyperbole, personification, alliteration and others can be found within the works of William Shakespeare. Define each of the following, find an example from the play, and then create your own example:

   a. Metaphor
   b. Simile
   c. Personification
   d. Alliteration

-

4. Another important aspect of any play is who is speaking and to whom. A character could be speaking to another character, themselves, or directly to the audience. Depending on who is being spoken to determine what other characters "know" about what is happening in the play. These are called soliloquies, monologues, and asides. Define them, give an example of each, and all write the significance of it for the overall direction of the play.

-

5. The idea of dreams and magic are prevalent throughout "A Midsummer Night's Dream". Is any of what you've read so far possible? What lessons are being taught in this way? Is it working?

-

Homework Assignments

-
- Links
-
- Figurative Language

- **http://languagearts.mrdonn.org/figurative.html**
- Figurative Language
- **http://www.slideshare.net/davygamm/literary-terms-in-a-midsummer-nights-dream**
-
-

1. **Collage**: Create a collage of modern-day symbols found in "A Midsummer Night's Dream". Accompany it with a 1 page explanation of why you chose the pictures you chose.
   -

2. **Making Connections**: Symbols are found in all parts of our life, not just the literature we read for school. Where else are symbols located (think of arrows and stop signs)? Why do you think we have universal symbols for various things? You will have to conduct some research to back up what you think.

3. **Bulletin Board (Poster):** Take each type of figurative language and create a picture board of them. Place the type (personification) at the top and below it a line or two from the play; below that a modern day version, and then either find a picture (or draw it) of a representation of each.

4. **Jeopardy**: Working with a partner, design a Jeopardy style game encompassing all you've learned about "A Midsummer Night's Dream," William Shakespeare, and Elizabethan England. You should have categories, double jeopardy, flash cards with questions, and don't forget to assign point values to the questions.

5. **Research Paper:** Choose a theme from the play to expand upon, a historical figure from Elizabethan England, or William Shakespeare to write research and write a paper about. Your paper will be 4-5 pages in length and follow MLA formatting guidelines.

6. **Scrapbook**: Create a scrapbook from Hermia or Helena's perspective; something she can show her family friends. Make sure have at least 5 pages.

7. **Social Media:** Design a social media page (FB, Twitter, Google+, etc.) for Puck, Lysander, Demetrious, Oberon, and Nick Bottom. How do you think social media would have changed their relationships or even the outcome of the story?

Day 5: What Makes it a Great Book?

-

Objective

-
- What makes "A Midsummer Night's Dream" a marvellous play? Could it be the timeless theme? Students will spend this lesson/session reviewing the play and deciding whether or not they do think it's a fantastic play and making connections to their world today to back up their thoughts and ideas.

-
- Students should complete reading through Act V for this lesson. They should also review the earlier acts in order to make connections.

-

Discussion Questions/Writing Journal Responses

-
1. Think back (or look back) to your first journal entry. Were all your questions answered about Shakespeare and about "A Midsummer Night's Dream"? If not, what questions do you still have? What have you learned that you didn't know before?
-
2. Now that you've read the entire play, is it easier to see the foreshadowing? Go back and make a list of any you may have missed.

3. In Act V of "A Midsummer Night's Dream" we have another play taking place (by the players who did not have time to practice because of Puck's interference. What is this story? Does it have any relevance to "A Midsummer Night's Dream" or could it have been left out? Explain.

4. Who is your favorite character and why? What would happen to the story if they were not in the play (or if they

died (or died earlier)? Could the play work without them? How?

5. We only catch glimpses of the parents in the play. Why do you think this is? With what little we do know, we've learned from others. Do you believe we have an accurate picture? What are your thoughts on the parents and their role?

   •

Homework Assignments

- •
  - Link
- Podcast on Arms
- **http://www.folger.edu/documents/Armor_podcast.mp3**
- Persuasive Essay Graphic Organizer
- **http://steckvaughnadult.hmhco.com/HA/correlations/pdf/ l/LEh5_graphicorg.pdf**
- Interactive Persuasive Guide
- **http://www.readwritethink.org/files/resources/interactive s/persuasion_map/**
- Crossword Puzzle
- **http://www.folger.edu/documents/Midsummer%20Cross %20Word.pdf**

1. **Modernize**: Choose your favorite scene from the play and rewrite it for today. Don't forget stage directions; costuming; and relationships.

   •

2. **Persuasion**: Write a persuasive essay on why you think "Romeo and Juliet" was a terrific read (or not so great). Why others should read it (or why not)? Use text to back up your opinion and don't forget to include a rebuttal of the opposition's argument, as well.

3. **Retraction**: Pretend Shakespeare's readers demanded he rewrite the ending of the play because they didn't like it.

Rewrite the ending so it becomes more dramatic or even a tragedy. Is it possible to only rewrite the ending?

4. **Nightly News**: With a small group prepare and deliver interviews with Theseus, Hippolyta, Oberon, and Titania. Create a nightly news bulletin or be the media at the "scene". Do you think there would have been more punishment doled out if there was a media presence like there is today?

5. **Time Lines**: Complete the timeline you began in Lesson 3. Is it realistic that this happened in such a short period of time?

6. **Replica**: In the first lesson, you designed the Globe Theatre. Here, you will create a replica (shadow boxes, for example) of one scene from each Act in "A Midsummer Night's Dream".

7. **Perform**: Choose either one monologue or one soliloquy and prepare to perform/recite it for the class. You must also describe the significance of the piece you chose and what the meaning of it is. This is a memorization piece, and you will not use notes (other than for meaning).

8. **Comic**: Recreate "A Midsummer Night's Dream" as a graphic novel or comic. You can either use typical Shakespearean characters and dialogue or you can modernize it. Make sure you are consistent throughout.

9. **Choose Your Own:** Choose your own project to complete. It must show your understanding of the entire play, and it must be approved by me before you begin.

10. **Playbill**: Do some research on what a playbill is and what they looked like during Elizabethan England. Design one for "A Midsummer Night's Dream".

•

Lesson Resources

•

Merriam-Webster's Collegiate Dictionary. Springfield, MA:

Merriam-Webster, 2001.

Pennington, Michael. *A Midsummer Night's Dream: A User's*

Guide. London: Nick Hern, 2005. Print.

Shakespeare, William. "A Midsummer Night's Dream : | :

Open Source Shakespeare. *A Midsummer Night's Dream*

: | : Open Source Shakespeare.. Open Source, 2003. Web. 27

Sept. 2012.

<http://www.opensourceshakespeare.org/views/play

s/playmenu.php? WorkID=midsummer>.

Shakespeare, William. *A Midsummer Nights Dream.*

Cambridge: University, 1936. Print.

Shakespeare, William. "Midsummer Night's Dream: Entire

    Play." *Midsummer Night's Dream: Entire Play.* MIT, 1993.

    Web. 27 Sept. 2012.

    <http://shakespeare.mit.edu/midsummer/full.html>.

Shurin, Aaron. *William Shakespeare's A Midsummer Night's*

    Dream. Woodbury, NY: Barron's Educational Series,

    1985. Print.

    •

Study Guide

Historical Context

William Shakespeare, playwright extraordinaire, lived in 16th to 17th Century England. He wrote an immense number of plays, including the still popular Hamlet, Macbeth, and Romeo & Juliet. Many of his plays were written as part of the Lord Chamberlain's Men—later known as the King's Men—who were a company of players, or actors. Although Shakespeare is synonymous with the Globe Theatre, a great number of his plays were performed at Blackfriars Theatre and at court for royalty and their guests. He was also a seasoned poet and is still celebrated for his 154 sonnets, including the popular Sonnet 18. The beginning lines are possibly the most quoted out of all the sonnets: "Shall I compare thee to a Summer's day? Thou art more lovely and more temperate." I bet you've heard those lines before!

The 16th and early 17th Centuries in England were periods of enormous wealth and strength. Shakespeare lived through the Spanish war, saw the end of Elizabeth the Virgin Queen's reign, and heralded in the reunification of the English and Scottish thrones under one monarch, King James VI. However, despite the Royal family's enormous wealth and rich noblemen in the upper classes, the poor were extremely poor. Famine, poor hygiene and the lack of wages created an environment full of disease, crime and pestilence. If you were poor during this time, you had mighty little to look forward to! Some would visit the theatre as a means to escape their lives if they could afford it, but they would only be able to afford standing room. Imagine standing up through an hour long play! Other entertainment available to the poor included watching executions, tormenting those placed in stocks and attending witch trials. A pretty grim past-time, but there was little else to do,

A Midsummer Night's Dream is still one of Shakespeare's most popular plays. Most historians believe that the play was written between the years 1590 and 1956, when it debuted on stage. It was performed secretly during the Puritan period that criticized and shut down plays rulers did not like at festivals and fairs. Once it was performed on main stages again, it did not gather many compliments due to its farcical and exaggerated style. Many thought it was a play best suited to being read on paper, rather than being performed on stage. This is due in part to the darned little character development and the sudden new direction for the play once the Mechanicals perform. Even Samuel Pepys, a famous member of Parliament at the time, called it a ridiculous play.

Usually, Shakespeare liked to touch on a specific source for his plays, but <u>A Midsummer Night's Dream</u> appears to be strangely without one. Despite this, the play references many texts, including his own <u>Romeo & Juliet</u>, and Chaucer's <u>Canterbury Tales</u>.

Despite criticisms that some have had, <u>A Midsummer Night's Dream</u> is still well loved and continues to be tweaked and adapted and performed. In the more modern world, the play has been adapted into ballet performances, musicals, films and has inspired many more fictional works. Its blend of the comic and fantasy are strong draws for many artists, especially those that have embellished and adapted the fairy world to enhance Shakespeare's work into a feast for the eyes!

Plot Overview

Short Synopsis

After given an ultimatum by her father, Egeus, and Theseus, the Duke of Athens, to marry Demetrius on their command or become a nun, Hermia and Lysander, her lover, run away into the woods. Helena, who is in love with Demetrius, decides to tell him where Hermia has gone to get his attention. At the same time, the warring monarchs of the fairy world — Titania and Oberon — quarrel over an Indian Boy. Their quarrel leads to mischief, trickery, misunderstandings. What follows in the Athenian woods is a chaotic love story that, unsurprisingly for a comedy, ends with three happy weddings and the reunification of the fairy world.

Detailed Synopsis

Theseus and Hippolyta discuss their impending wedding.
They are interrupted by Egeus, a nobleman, who asks Theseus
for his help with his daughter, Hermia. She refuses to marry
Demetrius, who Egeus has picked out for her and wants to
follow her heart and marry Lysander for love instead. Hermia
is told she must marry Demetrius or become a nun. Demetrius
and Lysander argue with one another; Lysander reveals that
Demetrius has led another woman, Helena, on, and now she is
in love with him.

Lysander begs Hermia to run away with him so they can
elope. They decide to meet in the Woods at night, and
Lysander leaves to avoid suspicion. Hermia tells Helena about
their plan. After Hermia leaves, Helena reveals that she is in
love with Demetrius and is jealous of Hermia's superior looks.
She thinks this is the reason Demetrius loves Hermia more
than he loves her. She decides to tell Demetrius about
Hermia's elopement to get in his finest books. Maybe, she
thinks, this will put her in a kinder light.

In the meantime, the Mechanicals—a group of workers in an amateur dramatics club—arrive at a space in Athens to rehearse their play together. Quince, the leader of the group, hands out parts. Bottom, who is to play the lead role of Pyramus in Pyramus and Thisbe, interrupts at every chance he gets to provide his opinion, or ask to play more roles than just the lead. Quince politely disagrees with him each time. The others—Flute, Snout, Snug, and Starveling—are handed their parts and bring up their insecurities with each. For example, Snug is worried he won't be able to remember his lines as the Lion, even though his lines are all roars! Once all the parts have been handed out, they decide to meet in the Woods away from everyone else so they can rehearse without being interrupted.

In the Woods, Robin Goodfellow and another fairy meet. They talk about the King and Queen of the fairy world arguing over a stolen Indian boy. Queen Titania refuses to hand him over to King Oberon. As a result, the natural world is in disorder: fog has spread across the land and crops refuse to grow. They reveal to each other that Titania and Oberon are both coming to the Woods. The Fairy wants Oberon to go away so he won't upset her Queen.

Titania and Oberon meet. Oberon asks her for the Indian boy. Titania refuses as the boy's mother was a dear friend of hers who died. She looks after him for her friend. Oberon wants her to be obedient, but Titania refuses him. Titania knows the only reason Oberon has returned to the Woods is to wish Theseus well in his marriage, and because Oberon is in love with Hippolyta. Titania tells her fairies to follow her, and they leave Oberon and Robin alone. Oberon asks Robin to fetch a flower hit with a stray bow from Cupid's arrow and bring it to him: he will use the flower juice to make Titania fall in love with the next thing she sees so he can take the boy from her.

As Robin fetches the flower, Demetrius enters the woods, followed by Helena. Neither sees Oberon as he hides from sight. Helena begs him to love her again, but Demetrius threatens to rape her. She doesn't care if he hurts her; she's already hurt by the fact that he won't pursue her. Demetrius threatens to leave her with the wild animals and escapes into the thick of the woods once more, Helena hot on his heels. Oberon promises Helena that she will be pursued by the end of the night.

Robin returns with the flower. Oberon tells him to smear it on the eyes of an Athenian youth in the Woods so that he will love her more than she loves him. Oberon leaves to smear the flower juice on Titania's eyes.

Titania asks her fairy court to sing her to sleep and stand guard while she sleeps. Once she has fallen asleep, all but one leaves to carry out errands. Oberon enters and smears the flower juice across her eyes. He tells her not to wake up until something disgusting comes near, and then to fall in love with it. Oberon leaves.

Lysander and Hermia stumble in. They are tired and lost in the Woods. They decide to lie down to rest for a while. Lysander wants to lie close to Hermia, but she tells him to be gentlemanly and sleep further away. Lysander disagrees — they are in love; their hearts are as one, and so they should sleep near one another. Hermia refuses once more, and Lysander gives in, although points out he only meant the suggestion innocently. They go to sleep.

Robin enters and smears the flower juice across Lysander's eyes and chastises Hermia for sleeping so closely to him.

Demetrius and Helena enter. Demetrius continues to threaten Helena's safety. She begs him to stay with her, even if it means killing her. Demetrius tells her that he'll leave her to the wild animals and runs away again. Helena is too tired to run after him and decides to lie down to sleep, but, before she can, she sees Lysander. He wakes up and immediately falls in love with her. Lysander wants to find Demetrius so he can kill him for Helena's heart. Helena thinks that Lysander is making fun of her. She runs away. Lysander tells the still sleeping Hermia not to wake up or follow him as she is too sweet for him now. He runs after Helena.

Hermia wakes after a terrifying nightmare in which her heart is being eaten by a snake, and finds herself alone. She calls out to Lysander, but he does not answer. Fearing the worst, she decides to try and find him.

The Mechanicals gather in the Woods for a rehearsal of the play. They discuss various elements in the play that they need — Moonshine and a Wall — and how best to represent these on stage. Bottom is also worried about using a sword on stage when Pyramus has to kill himself. He doesn't want to frighten the audience, and so they decide to write a Prologue to explain to the audience that the play isn't real. Snout is also worried about the Lion frightening the audience, and Bottom decides that he should speak to the audience instead of roar to reassure the ladies. Once these issues have been resolved, the actors start to rehearse. None of them are remarkably talented.

Robin enters and is at first upset that they are rehearsing so close to Titania, but is intrigued by the prospect of an entertaining play. He thinks that Bottom's Pyramus is the strangest portrayal he's ever seen, and follows him off "stage" behind some bushes. Bottom returns with a donkey's head instead of his own, transformed by Robin. The others flee frightened that the monster will attack them. Bottom thinks that they are trying to trick him into being upset and refuses to run away. He sings, which wakes Titania. She falls in love with him on sight. Bottom doesn't quite understand why she has fallen in love with him, but doesn't actually argue with her. Titania calls her most trusted fairies — Peaseblossom, Moth, Cobweb and Mustardseed — to take care of Bottom. They leave to go and sleep in a flowerbed.

Oberon wonders whether or not Titania has fallen in love with something horrid yet. Robin enters and reports that she has fallen in love with Bottom, who he has given a donkey's head, and the Athenian youth is also in love with Helena as requested. Oberon sees Demetrius and Hermia coming—Robin reveals he has never seen Demetrius before, and may have mixed up the Athenian men. Hermia thinks Demetrius has killed Lysander as there's no other reason why he would have left her, but Demetrius defends himself: he hasn't even seen Lysander. Hermia won't talk to him again and runs away into the woods. Demetrius doesn't want to go after her while she's upset and goes to sleep.

Oberon tells Robin off, sends him to fetch Helena, and smears flower juice across Demetrius' eyes so that he will fall in love with Helena. Demetrius wakes and declares his love for Helena when she enters. Helena believes that both of the Athenian men are in on the joke now, and is upset. Demetrius gives up on his claim for Hermia and tells Lysander to go marry her instead, but Lysander doesn't want her either.

Hermia enters and asks Lysander where he went. He followed his love: Helena. Helena accuses Hermia of persuading the boys to trick her, but Hermia doesn't understand. They quarrel with one another, and once Hermia realizes Lysander genuinely does mean what he says; she threatens to beat Helena up. Demetrius and Lysander, too, decide to duel for Helena's hand.

Helena tries to reason with Hermia--she loves Hermia. They grew up together! Hermia tells her to leave. Helena does, afraid that Hermia will attack her. Demetrius and Lysander leave to fight one another further away in the woods. Hermia doesn't know what to think anymore. She leaves.

56

Oberon blames Robin for the mess he's made. Robin assures him that he made a mistakes. Oberon asks Robin to make the Woods dark so the two Athenian men won't be able to see one another to fight, and imitate their voices to lure them away from one another. He gives Robin a new flower to smear across their eyes and undo the damage he has caused. When the youths wake up, they will think of the night as if it were all a dream. Oberon plans to do the same for Titania after she gives him the Indian boy. They have to work fast to complete the work before the impending sunrise!

Lysander and Demetrius, still trying to find one another, follow Robin around the Woods. He uses their voices to call to them alternately until they both grow tired. They both lie down to sleep. Helena and Hermia, in separate areas of the Woods, decide to sleep as well, exhausted and weary from the trying night. Robin smears the flower juice on Lysander's eyes to cure him and bids them all to find the one they truly love when they wake.

While the others sleep, Titania and Bottom enter with her fairies. She dotes on him, scratching his ears and threading flowers in his hair. Bottom wishes nothing more than to sleep, and so Titania tells her fairies to leave them alone, and curls up with Bottom in a flowerbed.

Oberon and Robin, hidden from view, talk about Oberon's meeting with Titania. He managed to persuade Titania to hand over the Indian boy with no problem. After he releases Titania from the spell — for Oberon wants her to see what a fool he has made of her — Oberon wants Robin to remove Bottom's donkey head. Titania wakes up and is horrified to find that she was in love with Bottom, and never wants to see him again. Robin gives Bottom his human head back. While the Athenians sleep, Oberon and Titania dance together. Oberon is overjoyed; he has Titania back and is convinced that there will be three weddings the next day. Robin interrupts them: the night is almost over! Oberon and Titania leave for the other side of the world to catch up with the night.

Theseus and Hippolyta enter with servants and Egeus. They talk about a epic hunt they have planned, and praise the ability of hunting dogs to bark loudly enough for it to echo off cliffs and trees. Theseus suddenly sees the Athenians sleeping on the ground. He wakes them up with the servants' horns. Theseus assumes they are out in the Woods because they knew Theseus would be there, but questions Lysander and Demetrius as to why two enemies could sleep so closely to one another. They have no idea how they got there, but do remember running into the woods. Although Egeus calls for Lysander to be arrested upon hearing he planned to elope with Hermia, Demetrius interrupts with his version of the events and proclaims his love for Helena. He doesn't know how exactly it has happened, but his love for Hermia seems to have disappeared. Theseus refuses to uphold Egeus' wish and will allow the two happy couples to marry one another. They give up on hunting now that the day is running into the afternoon, and head back to Athens for the weddings. All but the four Athenians leave; they're not sure if they're awake yet or not, but decide they must be if they all saw Theseus. They decide to compare dreams along the way to Athens.

After they leave, Bottom awakes. He can't put into words what he just experienced, but will get Quince to write it down for him.

Back in Athens, the Mechanicals lament the loss of Bottom. They don't know where he is, and assume he has been kidnapped. They're upset that the play won't be put on as Bottom was the only person fit to play Pyramus. While they compliment his characteristics, Snug arrives to tell the group that there have been three couples married that day. Bottom arrives! He won't tell them what happened to him just yet as they need to get ready for the play!

Theseus, Hippolyta and Philostrate discuss the strange things the Athenian youths have been saying. Theseus believes it sounds downright made up and blames love for their hallucinations. Hippolyta wonders if it wasn't a dream as their dreams were all the same.

Demetrius, Helena, Lysander and Hermia arrive. After an exchange of blessings, Theseus calls on Philostrate to list the entertainment he has planned for the wedding party. Theseus rejects a few — including a retelling of Hercules and the Centaurs — but asks to see Pyramus and Thisbe. Philostrate warns them against it as he watched them rehearse earlier; they were awful! Theseus still wants to see it, and so Philostrate leaves to fetch them. Hippolyta doesn't want to laugh at poor people, but Theseus assures her that they will be respectful and compliment what they do well.

The play begins. It's a bit of a shamble: the actors explain exactly what is happening on stage rather than acting out the story. After a brief Prologue telling the audience they are not there to entertain them, Pyramus and Thisbe talk through the Wall, played by Snout, who holds up his two fingers to form a chink in the wall. The two lovers plan to meet at Ninny's tomb. In a series of asides to one another, Hippolyta, Theseus and Demetrius criticize or compliment the actors. Hippolyta thinks this play is the silliest she's ever seen.

Snug as the Lion appears on stage and explains to them that he's not actually a Lion. The Moon enters, carrying a lantern and explains rather confusingly that he is the man in the moon and the lantern is the moon. Demetrius jokes that he would like to see how the man could fit into the lantern so easily, but the Moon continues on regardless. Meanwhile, Thisbe is frightened by the Lion, who tears her cloak off and rips it.

Pyramus finds Thisbe's cloak and assumes she has been killed and stabs himself with his sword. Hippolyta hopes Thisbe won't cry over Pyramus too much as he isn't truly worth it. Thisbe finds Pyramus and stabs herself. Breaking character, Bottom asks if the audience wants to hear the Epilogue, but Theseus thinks that a play where all the main characters have died doesn't need an Epilogue; there's no-one left to blame!

Theseus congratulates them on their performance, and then announces to the others that it is time for bed.

Robin steps in. He talks about the ghoulish and supernatural things that happen when night comes. He has been sent ahead to clean the house and make sure no one disturbs the sleeping Athenians before the fairies arrive. Oberon and Titania sing and dance together to bless the house, the marriages, and the couples' future children. They all leave but Robin, who addresses the audience. He asks them to think of the play as a kind of dream if it has offended them. If they give him a chance, he can set things right, and if he doesn't set things right he will be called a liar. He asks the audience to applaud if they are still friends, and then leaves.

Themes/Motifs

Forbidden Love

In Act One Scene One, Lysander discusses the ways that love has been forbidden throughout history, either through age difference or class separation. Hermia's love is forbidden by her father, Egeus. Helena's love is forbidden by her beloved Demetrius. Titania forbids Oberon to come near her again because of their quarrel and refuses to hand over the Indian boy. In The Mechanical's play, Thisbe and Pyramus are forbidden to see one another, and even lose their lives before they can be together.

Perception

The flower juice that is smeared on Lysander and Titania's eyes changes their view of the world. It even changes their heart. They no longer see what they saw before. The humans — aside from Bottom — never see the fairy world, even though Robin and Oberon are often watching over them. The moon, which provides light for many of them, does not help illuminate the woods while Robin teases and taunts Lysander and Demetrius through the shadows. They think they're following one another, but they're actually being tricked by Robin.

Foolishness

Bottom, even in his name, is quite a foolish character. Although many of the workmen putting on the play have moments of stupidity, Bottom's arrogance coupled with his utter ignorance paint him as a man who thinks he's the best at everything he attempts, when actually he's quite awful. That the others are duped into believing Bottom is a fantastic performer only adds to the comedy. When Bottom is given a donkey's head, he physically represents folly.

Later on the performers of the play do not even realize that they're performing incorrectly — i.e by explaining to the audience what is happening rather than showing them — and do not realize they are being mocked by Theseus and the rest of the audience. But it's not just Bottom who is an intensely foolish character; Hermia and Helena have an argument about their contrasting heights without Helena realising that she's picking on Hermia for it, and Demetrius can be called a fool for believing he loves Hermia enough to reject Helena, who he arguably knew he loved.

Reason and Love

When Bottom comments that reason and love do not go well together (3.1), he simplifies a common thread of investigation in the play. It seems that none of the players in <u>Midsummer</u> follow reason closely when faced with their love, or when following their heart's desire, and those that are questioned over their choice of love are often faced with statements others believe to be logical. For example, Egeus' attempts to control his daughter's heart are down to his role as a Father. Only when Theseus sees that there is no more claim on Hermia from Demetrius does he overrule societal law and let love win.

The mess that is made with the flower liquid suggests that love is illogical, ever changing, and can transform humans into blind, cruel people if they don't keep their heads. Even though it is reason that turns Hermia away into the woods, setting the events in action, and love that resolves their conflict, Theseus still rejects the lovers' remembrance of their dream as silly imagination. He rejects their memory in favour of reason. It is also reason that brings everything back under control, which suggests that maybe reason and love need to go together for a couple to survive.

Night and Day

Seeing by the light of the moon, or meeting under starlight might be considered romantic, but the night sky is actually indicative of the presence of the fairy world. Oberon admits that he does like the Sun, but he prefers to fly around at night. He also admits that their mischief must be undone and made right before daylight, suggesting some predetermined rules for their kind. When Titania meets with him, and the dawn comes, they leave for the darker side of the world. In many ways, the darkness of the night allows the fairies to cause mischief and fun. The day, and light, on the other hand, is the world of the humans. They wake at first light, and are in charge of what happens to them during this time, while the four Athenian youths and Bottom had no choice what was done to them throughout the night by the fairies.

Gender

Hermia and Helena threaten to attack one another over men despite the fact that they grew up together, and have obviously been close friends. They both fawn over the men that they love and chase them through the woods. Titania is tricked by her husband, Oberon, and made a fool of because she won't do as she is told when asked to give up the Indian boy. Despite the fact that Bottom has a donkey's head for much of the play, he seems less of a fool than Titania who calls him beautiful and embraces him in the flowerbeds. And Demetrius, though he chases Hermia into the woods to take her back from Lysander, threatens Helena with rape and murder if she doesn't stop following him. Even though she doesn't listen to him, his threats represent the distinct control men believe they have over women in this play.

The Dream World

A dreaming Hermia believes she sees Lysander sitting by as her heart is eaten, which is a strong metaphor for what has happened while she has been asleep. When she wakes up though, she has no idea where Lysander has gone. Just as the world is under a kind of fog, so too is reality. Titania wakes to find that she has had an awful dream about being in love with a donkey, and the Athenians remember the night in the woods as a dream under Oberon's command. It is in the world of dreams and the mystic that brings the most clarity.

The Supernatural

Although the Supernatural elements in the play can be blamed for the chaotic events and misunderstanding between the Athenians in the woods, magic ultimately resolves the problems between them and bring about a happy end for both couples. And, even though Oberon has to use magic to trick Titania into giving him the Indian boy, this resolves the argument between them and brings the natural world back to order once more.

Control and Manipulation

Egeus wants to control who his daughter, Hermia, marries. This way, he would be able to control not only her heart, but her body. Helena wants to control Demetrius and make him love her, just as Demetrius wants Hermia to love him, but Helena also suspects that it is Hermia who has manipulated the two men into pretending to love her. Although not revealed explicitly, its suggested that Hippolyta has been coerced into marrying Theseus because she lost the war to him; she isn't marrying him for love.

Peace and Chaos

Due to the war between Oberon and Titania, the seasons and weather are at odds with one another. Titania laments the loss of farmer's crops, and the fog that has crept over the world because of their fights. It seems that until the two fairy monarchs resolve their issues, the world will continue to be chaotic in nature. That chaos bleeds over into the other people in the play, especially the Athenian youths lost in the woods. In the human world, the threat Hermia represents is the undoing of the peace in her family by refusing to marry Demetrius at her father's command.

Character Summaries

Theseus (Fi-se-us)

Theseus is the Duke of Athens. Theseus himself may be based on the famous Greek God, who was the mythical King who founded Athens, and the total hero of the Athenian people. He is generally fair and just, because he overrides Egeus' wishes to force his daughter to marry Demetrius once the four lovers have sorted their problems out. He is also a man of law and society; he follows the rules of warfare in that he marries Hippolyta, and grants Egeus his initial request to force Hermia to decide between Demetrius and becoming a nun. However, he is also another example of the power that man has over woman in <u>Midsummer</u>, for he has not won Hippolyta's heart and hand in marriage honourably, but in the battlefield.

Hippolyta (Hip-pol-li-ta)

Hippolyta, the Queen of the Amazons, is due to marry Theseus after she and her army were defeated in battle. We don't see or hear much from her, probably due to her subserviency to Theseus after she has lost the war, but what we do find out is that she is mildly protective of the common man. This could be because she feels uncomfortable around them. She comments that she doesn't want to watch the play if they're going to mock the actors for their own entertainment. This could be Shakespeare's way of using the female presence as a place of sympathy, but it could also be due to her empathy as someone who has been trapped.

Lysander (Li-san-der)

Lysander is in love with Hermia and will not stand down despite the threats to his safety made by Demetrius and Hermia's father, Egeus. It can be assumed that Lysander is quite romantic, as he not only discusses numerous forbidden loves, but also wants to steal Hermia away into the night to elope with her. Lysander seems used to using his soft and gentle manner to persuade people into giving him what he wants, as he tries this with Hermia when they lie down together in the wood. When he is threatened by Demetrius, however, his masculine nature appears once more, suggesting that masculinity is the stronger of the sexes.

Demetrius (De-me-trius)

Demetrius is a bit of a scoundrel: he fell in love with Helena, and then changed his mind and decided he wanted Hermia instead. He threatens Helena in the woods after she chases him with not only rape, but also death. He leaves her alone in the woods to fend for herself because he wants to find Hermia, and yet through all this Helena sticks by him. He also joins in with the criticisms of the play with Theseus, so it can be assumed — although we don't see much evidence of it — that he is always looking for the Duke's approval. Either that, or Demetrius just majorly enjoys being nasty.

Helena (*Hel-ena*)

An Athenian lady. It would be an understatement to say that Helena suffers from low self esteem; she constantly puts herself down because of her physical attributes, and for her personality. She claims she cries too much and blames this on her poor features. She grew up with Hermia and has probably been in quiet competition with her since they met, as her fears and insecurities appear unusually deep seated. Helena is extremely love-sick for Demetrius, who she was engaged to before he fell in love with Hermia. Even though her loyalty to Demetrius can be seen as a sign of weakness, especially when he threatens to rape her, she shows her cleverness in the plan to get him back through giving him information, and in her refusal to believe Lysander loves her.

Hermia (Her-mia)

The second of the Athenian ladies, Hermia is well loved by all. She is called beautiful, so we can assume that she has had many suitors, from which Demetrius has been chosen for her. She's forthright in her belief that she should be able to marry for love, and is brave enough to take what would be a terrifying step away from her father and everything she knows for love.

Titania

The Queen of the Fairies, Titania starts off as a strong ruler who will not bow to her husband's wishes due to her morality. She will not give up the Indian Boy just because he wants him, and has made a vow to her friend and the boy's mother. And yet, after Titania is made a fool of, and she is tricked into handing back the Indian Boy, she takes Oberon back without much any argument. From then on, she takes his orders, dances with him and is generally amenable. Although it could be argued that this is evidence of male dominance, it could also represent Titania's nurturing side. She refuses to follow Oberon's orders because her maternal instincts tell her not to, and once she no longer has to worry for the boy; she can forgive Oberon easily.

Robin (Puck)

Robin, or Puck as he is often known, is a complete mischief maker and the trickster personified. He is a servant to Oberon and is sent to fetch flowers, run errands and smear the flower juice across the Athenian youth's eyes. Robin, in essence, gets many of the events of the play rolling and is quite a prominent character for this reason. Some historians have even pinpointed Robin as the protagonist of <u>Midsummer</u> as the play is without a clear lead. Although he plays cruel tricks on Bottom by giving him a donkey's head, he is generally a kindhearted character and will admit to mistakes he has made. Robin is a fairy, but he is not as gentle and sweet as Titania's servants; instead, he is a little more rough around the edges.

Oberon

The King of the Fairies. He, like Theseus and Egeus, believe that they can and should be able to control their wives, and is gobsmacked that his wife, Titania, continues to refuse him. He does not take delight in mischief that is not specifically designed by him or goes against true love; for example, Robin pours the flower juice on the wrong person's eyes. If the mischief is advantageous to him-for example when getting the Indian Boy back-he delights in it as long as they follow the rules of their world.,

Egeus (Eh-gee-us)

Hermia's father, and an Athenian courtier. He wants to control his daughter as per societal law to force her to marry the person he has chosen for her. He looks to Theseus a lot for help in these matters, but concedes to his rule once he is told Hermia will marry the person she loves.

The Mechanicals

Nick Bottom

Bottom is a well respected man among his peers, even if those peers are not to be well respected by the audience of Midsummer. They believe he is the smartest and best looking among them, which of course means he will end up with the lead in the play. Bottom interrupts Quince constantly to preen and prattle on about his abilities as a speaker or dramatist, which doesn't lend him much respect from the reader. We're meant to laugh at him. When Robin watches him rehearse Pyramus' role, he is called a strange and stupid actor; Robin's immediate thought is to give him a donkey's head, an animal which is often used to represent foolishness. Despite his ignorance, Bottom does mean well, and the rest of the group do look to him for help, which he is always there to provide.

Peter Quince

Quince is the real leader of the drama group, and a carpenter by trade. He knows how to deal with Bottom's constant interruptions and attempts to take over direction either by changing the subject, asking Bottom directly for his advice or by refusing his suggestion wholly through compliments. For instance, Quince tells Bottom he is the only one who could play Pyramus, and so he couldn't possibly play other characters. A terrifically skilled manipulator! Beyond this, not much else is known about his character.

Francis Flute

Flute is a bellows-mender and plays Thisbe in the play at the end. He is reluctant to play a female character and claims this is because he has a beard coming (1.2.40-41) and doesn't want to shave it off. Quince waves him off and tells him that he'll wear a mask over his face, and that's that. Flute doesn't argue much, and when he does speak it is usually to worry or compliment someone. He appears to be quite a nervous person.

Snug

Snug, the joiner, plays the Lion and is excited by the prospect. He is, however, afraid of frightening the ladies in the audience, which shows his gentleness and sensitivity. Snug can be seen as another foolish character, as he is initially worried he won't be able to learn his lines — which are at the time all roars! He is the only minor character of the Mechanicals not given a first name.

Tom Snout

Snout, the tinker, plays the Wall in the play. Initially he is meant to play Pyramus' father, but the play's need for a Wall ended up being greater. He, like his friends and fellow actors, is terrified by the prospect of Bottom being transformed, but is one of only two to return and approach Bottom for a short while. Snout's bravery is short lived, however, as once he has pointed out Bottom's transformation, he flees to safety.

Scene Summaries

Act One

Act One, Scene One

In Athens, surrounded by an attending court including
Philostrate, an official, Theseus, the Duke of Athens and
Hippolyta, Queen of the Amazons, discuss their upcoming
wedding. They will measure the days left by the waxing of the
moon: they have four days before their marriage takes place.
Theseus has captured Hippolyta after he defeated the
Amazons in a fierce battle; now that he has defeated her with
his sword, he intends to defeat her in other ways. With love!

Theseus asks Philostrate to make the Athenian youths happy,
and draw them out of their sadness. He leaves to do so. As
Theseus continues to express his promises to Hippolyta, they
are interrupted by visitors. It is Egeus, an Athenian courtier,
with his daughter, Hermia, and her two suitors. He begs for
Theseus to force his daughter to marry Demetrius, who he has
given permission to marry his daughter. The only problem is
that Hermia is in love with Lysander, who Egeus claims has
put a spell over his daughter to make her disobey him. He
accuses Lysander of pretending to be in love with Hermia,
and then asks Theseus for his right as a father: to either force
Hermia to marry Demetrius or to kill her for her disobedience.

Theseus asks for Hermia's opinions but warns her to think carefully because Egeus is her father, and should be a God to her. Hermia claims Lysander is as worthy as her father is and wishes that he could see things from her point of view, but Theseus chastises her for this — she must see things from her father's perspective. Theseus tells her to think carefully about her decisions: either she will be locked away as a pure and holy nun, or die a happily married woman. Hermia would rather be locked away than lose her virginity to a man she doesn't love. Theseus gives her time to think: by the time he and Hippolyta marry she has to decide between becoming a nun, death, and marrying Demetrius.

Lysander and Demetrius argue between themselves. Lysander tells him to go marry Egeus as he loves Demetrius so much. Lysander begs Egeus to see his side: he loves Hermia, which should count for more than what Demetrius can provide. He reveals Demetrius has been seeing Helena and now Helena loves him! Theseus admits he had heard about this, but had not had time to ask Demetrius yet. Theseus asks Demetrius and Egeus to come with him to talk about something and gives Hermia a final warning to think about her decision. Everyone leaves but Lysander and Hermia.

Lysander comments on Hermia's pale face. She is upset. Lysander tells her not to worry — that throughout history love has overcome many obstacles. Lysander reminds her that sometimes love has to overcome differences in class, or age, or relies on the opinions of others. Hermia thinks these are all awful things to have to face, but stand as enough reason for them to fight for their love too. Hermia and Lysander plan to meet each other in the woods the following night so they can run away to his Aunt's house and marry.

Helena comes in. They politely disagree with one another as to which of them is the most beautiful. Helena is upset that Demetrius prefers Hermia and is jealous of her beauty, voice, and eyes. She would give the entire world to have Demetrius for herself. She asks Hermia's advice for how to get Demetrius' attention, but Hermia doesn't actually know what she's done; she frowns at him and he still loves her! Helena wishes she could smile as well as Hermia frowns! Helena blames Hermia's beauty for Demetrius refusing to pay her any attention. Hermia tells her not to worry; she won't be around for too much longer as she and Lysander are running away! She and Lysander tell Helena exactly where they will be meeting. Hermia asks her to pray for them and hopes she and Demetrius finally fall in love, and then disappears, claiming she and Lysander can't be seen together just in case they are found out. Lysander then leaves.

By herself, Helena laments her situation. She knows other people in Athens think she is just as pretty as Hermia, but it doesn't matter because Demetrius doesn't think so. They are both obsessed with someone they can't have. She is upset that Demetrius promised to love her forever before he met Hermia, and so to get back at her, she'll tell Demetrius about their plan to run away and elope. Hopefully Demetrius will be grateful to her for the information, which will be worth it in her fight against her rival, Hermia.

Act One, Scene Two

The artists who will perform at Theseus and Hippolyta's wedding party rehearse. Quince, Snug, Bottom, Flute, Snout and Starveling gather together and listen as Quince hands out positions in the play. Bottom generally interrupts at every possible moment. He asks Quince to tell them the name of the play, which is <u>A Very Tragic Comedy About the Horrible Deaths of Pyramus and Thisbe</u>. Bottom will play the title role of Pyramus, who kills himself for love.

Bottom claims he will make the audience cry endlessly, bids Quince to name the other actors, and then interrupts to deliver his lines. Bottom believes his performance was truly inspirational. Quince doesn't respond and continues to carry on giving out the parts to the actors. Flute is to play Thisbe, Pyramus' lover, but he doesn't want to because he has a beard growing. Quince tells him that he can wear a mask, which prompts Bottom to ask to play Thisbe, as well as Pyramus, wearing a mask when required. Quince refuses: he'll play Pyramus, no one else. Quince gives out the rest of the roles: Robin as Thisbe's mother, Snout as Pyramus' father, Quince as Thisbe's father and Snug in the part of the Lion.

Snug is worried he won't be able to learn his lines, but Quince assures him all he needs to do is roar. Bottom wants to play the Lion as well because he'll roar so well that the Duke will ask him to roar again. Quince believes his roar might scare the Duchess and her ladies; they would be put to death! Bottom will roar gently then. Quince once again tells him that he will play the part of Pyramus and no other because he's the only one who could play such a handsome man. Bottom finally agrees to just play Pyramus and asks Quince what kind of beard he should have, but Quince doesn't genuinely care. Bottom lists the different kinds of beards he could have, but Quince points out that not all French people have beards, and he could play it clean shaven.

Quince hands out the scripts and asks them to learn their lines by the next night, and meet him in the woods a mile out of town in the moonlight. This is to avoid people interrupting or watching them while they rehearse. He asks them not to fail him. Bottom promises that they will be there and work hard. Quince tells them to meet by the giant oak tree in the Duke's woods. They leave.

Act Two

Act Two, Scene One

In the wood near Athens, a Fairy and Robin Goodfellow meet. Robin asks her where she is going; she tells him that she has gone everywhere. She works for Titania, the Fairy Queen. She bids him farewell as the Queen and her followers will arrive soon. Robin warns her that King Oberon is planning to throw a party in the area that night, and that she should keep the Queen away. He's upset with her because she's stolen a boy from an Indian King, and Oberon wants the boy to accompany him while they travel through the wild forests. The Queen, he reveals, has refused to give him the boy, and now they won't talk to each other.

The Fairy asks if he's Robin Goodfellow, who she has heard of. She accuses him of being mischievous, scaring the ladies in the nearby village, keeping people lost at night and stealing the cream from the top of milk. She reveals he is also sometimes called Puck, or Hobgoblin, and those who call him these names receive virtuous deeds from him. Robin admits it: he tells jokes to Oberon, pretends to be a stool and makes people fall over, and generally takes part in mischief. He announces Oberon is approaching. The Fairy wishes he would go away because Titania is also arriving.

On either sides of the wooded area, Titania and Oberon enter with their courts. They are not pleased to see each other. Titania asks her Fairies to make Oberon leave, but he makes them wait a moment; surely she should be obedient to her husband? She points out that if she has to be faithful to him, then he should be faithful to her, and not spend his days in the fields with other girls. Titania goes on to point out that the only reason he has returned is to wish Theseus well in his marriage to Hippolyta, who was once his own love. Oberon is shocked that she hasn't bothered to mention her own love for Theseus. She has even interfered in Theseus' past love life to break up his relationships!

Titania points out that their constant bickering has had an enormous impact on the world around them: fogs have risen up, and corn has rotted, diseases are rife, no one sings anymore, and the seasons have changed their characteristics. Oberon promises that all these wrongs will be put right as long as she hands over the Indian boy to him. The boy's mother was a follower and friend of Titania's and died during childbirth, and so she takes care of him instead for her sake. Oberon asks Titania how long she intends on staying in the woods. She will only stay until after Theseus is married. After Oberon once again asks for the boy, Titania calls her fairies to follow her away from this place otherwise she will continue to argue with him.

Oberon asks Robin to fetch him a flower hit by a stray arrow from Cupid's bow that was aimed at a woman under a vow of chastity. Liquid from the flower when smeared on the eyelids of a sleeping person will make a man or woman fall in love with the next person they see. Oberon wants this done fast; Robin will move fast enough to circle the earth in 40 minutes!

Robin leaves Oberon alone. In an aside, Oberon reveals that plans to use this on Titania to make her fall in love with the next thing she sees so that he can take the Indian boy from her. He doesn't even care if she falls in love with a bull, wolf or lion! Hearing Demetrius and Helena approaching, Oberon makes himself invisible.

Demetrius tells Helena to go home and stop pursuing him — he doesn't love her. He is looking for Lysander and Hermia, but is finding it difficult to find them. Helena will love him no matter what he does, despite how unworthy she thinks she is. Demetrius warns her that she is in a difficult and dangerous situation with a man she should not trust: he could rape her and take her virginity. Helena does not think of herself as alone because he is the entire world to her. Demetrius threatens to run away from her and leave her to wild animals. She'll still run after him. Demetrius begs her to leave him alone, and once again threatens to hurt her. Helena tells him that he's already hurt her — women, she believes, aren't meant to pursue men, but to be pursued! Demetrius leaves, followed by Helena who doesn't mind if she dies by the hand of the person she loves.

Oberon promises Helena she'll be the one who is pursued by the end of the night. Robin returns with the flower. He describes a place covered with growing flowers where Titania sleeps. Oberon will go there and smear a little part of the flower onto her eyelids. He gives a part of the flower to Robin and asks him to spread it across an Athenian man's eyes so that the next thing he'll see is Helena. He wants it done so that he'll love her more than she loves him. They leave, going in separate directions.

Act Two, Scene Two

Titania enters with her Fairies. She asks them to sing her to sleep before they go off to complete their work. They do, warning away snakes and other nasty things while their Queen sleeps. One of them stands guard over her while the others fly away to do their work.

Oberon enters and smears the flower juice across Titania's eyelids. He tells her to fall in love with the first thing that she sees when she wakes up, and bids her to wake up only when something nasty wanders by her. Oberon leaves.

Lysander and Hermia enter. He admits that he doesn't know where they are and is worried about how pale Hermia is. He suggests that they rest for a while to regain their strength, which Hermia agrees to. She'll sleep against a tiny hill, and tells Lysander to find something to sleep against, as well. Lysander disagrees; they'll sleep against the hill together because their love makes them one. Hermia isn't so sure she wants Lysander so close and asks him to sleep further away. Lysander assures her that he only meant it innocently. He believes that two hearts that love each other can be seen as one heart. They are connected by their vow of faith and should sleep close by. Hermia once again refuses: she wants to behave as they should. She is, however, thankful for his love, and wishes that it will always be this strong for her. Lysander agrees, and the two go to sleep.

Robin enters, still trying to find the Athenian youth to smear the flower juice on. He sees Lysander and Hermia and realizes that they must be the people he's been looking for. He smears the juice across Lysander's eyes and chastises Hermia for sleeping so close to someone so cruel. Robin adds another charm to the juice to prevent Lysander from being able to sleep again because of his overwhelming love. Robin leaves to find Oberon.

Demetrius enters, chased by Helena, who begs him to stay still even if it's to kill her. Demetrius tells her to leave, but Helena is afraid of being left alone. He couldn't possibly leave her alone in the woods! Demetrius leaves, telling her to find her own way as he's going to continue trying to find Hermia.

Helena is exhausted from chasing Demetrius. She wonders aloud how Hermia's eyes are so much brighter than hers — she assumes its because Hermia does not need to cry as much, whereas she is always upset. She compares herself to a bear, as even beasts run away from her in fear when they meet; of course Demetrius would run away from her when she looks like a monster. Suddenly she sees Lysander lying on the ground. After a brief moment of fear that he is actually dead, she bids Lysander wake up.

He does — when he sees Helena he proclaims his love for her! Lysander wonders where Demetrius is for he wants to run a sword through him and kill him. Helena tells him that he doesn't need to kill Demetrius because Hermia loves him, and for that he should be happy. Lysander doesn't understand why he would be happy with Hermia. To him, she's boring. It's more than logical to love Helena more than Hermia. His reason now guides him instead of his desire, and now he can see all love stories in her eyes.

Instead of believing him, Helena thinks he's making fun of her. She is upset that not only will she never be able to have Demetrius, but that Lysander has to treat her like this. She thought Lysander was much kinder than this. Before she leaves, she once again tells him that it is terribly cruel for a man to emotionally abuse her after another has already rejected her. She flees.

Lysander realizes that Helena had not seen Hermia. He begs Hermia not to wake up or come near him again—she is too sickly sweet for him to stomach anymore. Citing the fact that it was a complete mistake to ever fall in love with Hermia, he'll work hard to find Helena and serve her. He leaves.

Hermia wakes up, thick in the middle of a nightmare about a snake eating her heart while her beloved Lysander watched on. She calls out for Lysander, who is not there. She calls again, but he does not answer. Hermia decides to find him, or die in the process.

Act Three

Act Three, Scene One

As Titania sleeps on, Quince and the other players gather. Bottom checks that they are all present. They are. Quince proclaims that this area is perfect for their rehearsals, and they will practice the play in full before they perform in front of the Duke. Bottom, as always, interrupts. He's worried that some things in the play won't work. For instance, Pyramus has to kill himself with a sword, but he's concerned this will upset the ladies in the audience. Some of them agree, and fear they will have to leave out all the killing, but Bottom has an idea. He wants to recite a prologue to assure the audience that no one is going to be hurt during the play and that they're not actually Pyramus and Thisbe, and so on, but actors playing the parts. Quince agrees, but he and Bottom disagree regarding the number of syllables in the lines that will be written.

Snout is still worried the Lion will scare the ladies. Bottom agrees: there's nothing scarier than a Lion! Snout suggests adding another Prologue, but Bottom won't have that. Snout will simply show his face in the costume's neck, and talk directly to the audience to let them know he isn't a real Lion.

Quince is worried about the moonlight they will need to bring into a room as Thisbe and Pyramus meet by moonlight. Snout asks if the moon will be shining that night. They gather a calendar to double check: thankfully, it is. Bottom suggests leaving a window open for the light to come through. Quince agrees and then suggests an actor holding a lantern could also represent the moon. But there's another problem: Thisbe and Pyramus are meant to speak through a hole in the wall, so where will they find a wall? Bottom suggests someone plays the Wall so that Thisbe and Pyramus can speak through the Wall's fingers. Quince is satisfied now. He starts the rehearsal, asking anyone not on stage at the time to hide in the bushes until their cue comes.

Robin enters. At first he is afraid that these men are so close to the sleeping Titania, but when he sees they are rehearsing a play he decides to watch, and might join in if the mood takes him. Bottom as Pyramus gets some of his words incorrect — he exchanges "odious" for "odours" and so on. Robin is appalled: he's never seen a stranger Pyramus. As Bottom leaves the stage, Robin follows him. Flute as Thisbe recites all of his lines at once in a rush and even reads the cues!

Robin and Bottom return. Bottom now has a donkey's head instead of his own! Quince and the others run for their lives, afraid of being attacked by this monster. Bottom doesn't understand why they run from him. Robin promises to make Bottom's life a hard one by getting him lost and turning himself into beasts to frighten Bottom with. Snout returns and asks him what he has on his head, then leaves. Quince returns to to bless him and leaves too.

Bottom is suspicious. He thinks they're trying to frighten him into making a fool of himself, but he'll refuse to do such a thing. He'll even sing a song to prove to them that he's not afraid. Titania wakes up. Once Bottom stops singing, Titania begs him to sing again. She loves to look at him, and even though this is the first time she's seen him, she can't help but tell Bottom she loves him. Bottom doesn't see much reason for her to love him, but then he's sure that love and reason don't certainly have much to do with one another anyway. Titania tells him that he is as wise as he is beautiful. Bottom disagrees. If he were exceedingly wise, he'd be out of the woods already. Titania tells him that he can't leave — she won't let him. She loves him. She and her fairy servants will serve him, and give him immortality. Titania calls for her fairies by name: Peaseblossom, Cobweb, Moth, and Mustardseed.

They enter and ask what Titania would have them do. She asks them to be kind to Bottom, to give him food to eat and light to sleep by, and to use butterfly wings to block moonlight getting in his eyes. Bottom asks for their names and awkwardly introduces himself. For instance, he tells Mustardseed he is sorry that most of his family will have been smeared on beef. Titania tells the fairies to take him away so he can sleep. She believes the moon looks sad: either this is because someone is not being loved, or someone is being forced to love without their will. She wants Bottom brought to her quietly.

Act Three, Scene Two

Oberon wonders if Titania is awake yet, and what she has ended up in love with if she is awake. Robin enters. Oberon demands a report on what mischief he has made. He tells Oberon that Titania is in love with a monster, which he created by putting a donkey's head on the bumbling, stupid one playing Pyramus. His friends ran away and were frightened by everything they came across, even bristles and thorns. Robin led them on as trees and bushes pulled on their hats and sleeves. Then, Titania woke up and fell in love with Bottom. Oberon is mightily pleased.

He asks if Robin put the flower juice on the eyes of the Athenian youth as asked. Robin has, and is positive that he will have seen the girl when they woke up as they slept near one another. Oberon tells him to be quiet as the Athenian is approaching. Robin tells Oberon that it is the same woman, but not the same man he saw.

Demetrius and Hermia enter. He doesn't understand why she is so angry with him when he loves her so much. She's upset that he might have killed Lysander while he was asleep. She doesn't believe he would have left her because he's been so faithful to her, so something must have happened to him. She argues that it is obvious that Demetrius has killed Lysander because he looks so pale and grim. Demetrius argues that he looks pale and grim because she is murdering his spirit with her cruel words. Hermia demands to know what he has done with Lysander. Demetrius assures her he didn't kill Lysander, nor does he think Lysander is even dead. Hermia begs him to tell her Lysander is alright, but Demetrius wouldn't get much out of that. Hermia agrees he won't get far with her: she'll never see Demetrius again, even if she never sees Lysander again. She leaves. Demetrius can't go after her while she's this upset, so he decides to lie down and sleep.

Oberon chastises Robin — he's put the flower juice on the wrong person's eyes! He's undone true love, and made false love true! Robin doesn't care much as he believes it is down to fate for love to be so confusing. Oberon orders him to fly through the woods and find Helena, and bring her to Oberon so he can put a charm on her eyes. Robin leaves.

Oberon smears the flower juice across Demetrius' eyes. He hopes that when he sees the girl he's supposed to love he will remember how he feels. Robin announces that Helena is nearby with Lysander, who is begging her to love him. They decide to watch quietly. Robin is excited to watch two men in love with the same woman; this is one of his favourite predicaments.

Lysander and Helena enter first. Lysander doesn't understand why Helena thinks he's making fun of her because he's crying when he tells her that he loves her. People don't cry when they tease someone! Helena still doesn't believe him, because he's made the same promises to both her and Hermia now, and as they can't both be true promises then they have to be false ones. Lysander assures her he wasn't thinking clearly when he made those promises to her. Helena still doesn't believe he's thinking clearly now as he breaks his promises to Hermia, but Lysander doesn't care. Demetrius loves Hermia and can have her.

Demetrius wakes up and proclaims his love for Helena. He calls her beautiful, comparing her lips to cherries, the pure white snow of the mountain as black next to her pale hand. He wants to kiss her hand as it would make him so happy. Helena is upset that they're both now ganging up on her to pretend they love her. She wants them just to hate her again as she knows they do. If they were real men, they would treat her kindly. Not only are they competing for Hermia's love, they're now competing to mock her. Not a manly thing to do at all!

Lysander asks Demetrius not to be cruel: they all know Demetrius loves Hermia. Lysander gives up all claims and love for her in exchange for Demetrius giving up on his claim for Helena. But, Demetrius doesn't want Hermia; he only wants Helena. His love for Hermia was only temporary. Lysander and Demetrius continue to fight with one another until Hermia arrives. She tells them that, even though its hard to see at night, it's much easier to hear, and this is how she has managed to find Lysander — by following his voice. She asks him why he left her by herself, when surely his love for her would have told him to stay. It is his love for Helena that told him to leave! Lysander doesn't understand why she doesn't know that he hates her. Helena is upset that all three of them are in on the plot to mock her. Helena begs Hermia to remember that they grew up together, and are extremely alike. She asks Hermia to remember their vows of friendship. She also reminds Hermia that it isn't lady-like to do what she is doing.

Hermia is thoroughly confused. It sounds, she says, like Helena is insulting her, not the other way around. Helena pushes her to confess that she sent Lysander and Demetrius to find and praise her beauty and confess their love. It makes no sense for Lysander to have rejected Hermia, so of course Hermia has to be involved somehow. Helena doesn't understand why Hermia hates her so much, when actually she should be pitied for being so unlovable. Hermia still doesn't understand what Helena is talking about. Helena tells her to continue with her little game if she pleases — maybe, she suggests, she should even write a book about it! Helena blames herself for being fought over. She shouldn't have followed them into the woods. Either leaving or dying will solve that problem.

Lysander begs her to stay and listen to him. Hermia tells Lysander not to insult Helena, and Demetrius threatens Lysander to stop. Lysander refuses to listen to either of them because he loves Helena. They argue over who loves her more. They decide to duel with one another to prove who loves Helena more. Hermia tries to pull Lysander back, but he tries to throw her off. Demetrius teases him for not fighting with him and pretending Hermia is holding him back. He calls Lysander a coward. Lysander calls Hermia a thorn and tries to shake her off. Hermia is confused — is he joking? Of course he is, Helena tells her, and so is she. Lysander is ready to fight Demetrius as promised once he has shaken Hermia off. Demetrius teases him once again for not upholding his promises terribly often. Lysander doesn't know what to do to prove his hate for Hermia beyond insults; he won't attack or kill her, if that's what Demetrius wants. Hermia finally realizes that Lysander means what he says. She cries out to God to help her.

Hermia turns on Helena, calling her a snake for stealing her beloved Lysander's heart in the night. Helena, in return, argues that Hermia is still pretending with Lysander and Demetrius. She calls Hermia a "puppet". Hermia interprets that to mean she is short and comes to the conclusion that Helena has shown off her height to the boys to make them like her more than the shorter Hermia. Hermia isn't too short to gouge Helena's eyes out though! Helena turns to the boys once more and begs them to stop Hermia from attacking her.

Helena assures Hermia that she loves her, and the only horrible thing she did to Hermia is tell Demetrius about her elopement with Lysander. And the only reason why she did this was because she loves Demetrius so much. She admits she's been foolish, and will return to Athens. Hermia tells her to go, then, but Helena's "foolish heart" keeps her standing still. Hermia wants clarification just who she's leaving her heart with; Helena answer is, of course, with Demetrius. Lysander and Demetrius assure Helena that they won't let Hermia hurt her. Helena refers to their time at school together, where Hermia was a fierce fighter despite being little. Hermia loses her temper over her height being mentioned again.

Demetrius and Lysander leave to fight one another. Hermia blames the duel on Helena, and tells her to stay where she is, but Helena doesn't trust her not to attack her runs away. Hermia doesn't know what to think anymore and leaves too.

Oberon blames Robin for this mess. He doesn't know if Robin did this on purpose or by accident. Robin assures his King that he made a mistake. Oberon had told him that he'd be able to recognize the Athenian youth by his clothes, which is what he did. Robin finds all of this amusing anyway. Oberon is worried that the two men will start to fight and asks Robin to make the sky overcast and as dark as hell so they won't be able to find one another. Then, he bids Robin to imitate the men and call out to them to keep them moving so they can try to fight and tire themselves out. Eventually they will fall to the ground to go to sleep.

Oberon gives Robin a new flower. He tells Robin to smear the flower juice on Lysander's eyes to undo all the damage that has been caused. When they wake up, the night will seem like a dream, and they can then return to Athens. He'll do the same for Titania if she promises to give him the Indian boy. Robin knows they have to work fast as dawn is approaching, and the ghosts of the people who committed suicide are travelling back to their graveyards after wandering around all night. Oberon reminds Robin that they aren't those kind of spirits and that he loves the sunlight, but agrees that a swift resolution before daylight would be for the best. Oberon leaves.

Lysander and Demetrius enter and exit, trying to find one another and are led around by Robin imitating them both. Eventually, Lysander ends up in a dark space and decides to lie down to rest until the early morning light lets him find Demetrius. Demetrius also lies down, equally exhausted by chasing the fake Lysander around. Helena enters and, wanting to escape her troubles for a while, goes to sleep. Robin knows there should be a fourth. Hermia finally appears, intensely weary and upset. She hopes to find Lysander safe and alive, but can't go any further tonight. She goes to sleep. Robin smears the flower juice on Lysander's eyes and tells them to find the woman they honestly love when they wake up.

Act Four

Act Four, Scene One

While Demetrius and the others still sleep, Titania and Bottom enter with her fairy court. Oberon watches them, hidden from sight. She asks Bottom to sit down so she can place flowers in his hair and rub his cheeks. Bottom asks the fairies to scratch his head and bring him honey. Titania wonders if he'd like to hear some music, or have something distinctive to eat. What Bottom would actually like to do is to sleep. He asks that no one wake him. The fairies leave. Titania puts her arms around Bottom to protect him in sleep, tells Bottom she loves him mightily and goes to sleep.

Robin enters. Oberon tells him that he actually feels sorry for Titania. He met her while she was gathering flowers for Bottom's head and, after arguing with her and insulting her, he asked for the Indian boy, which she gladly agreed to. She sent him over with one of her fairies. Now that Oberon has what he wants, he'll release Titania from the spell, and Robin will take the donkey's head from Bottom. They'll only remember this like an unpleasant dream. Oberon squeezes the flower juice on Titania's eyes.

Titania wakes up, afraid because she had an awful dream that she was married to a donkey. Oberon points to Bottom; Titania is shocked! She doesn't want to look at Bottom's face again. Oberon tells her to be quiet while Robin removes Bottom's donkey head. He asks Titania to get the fairies to play music so the sleeping Athenians will continue to sleep soundly. After removing Bottom's donkey head, Robin tells him to see once again through his own foolish eyes.

Oberon asks Titania to dance with him, and she actually agrees! Now that they're together again, Oberon suggests they should dance together for the Duke at his wedding to bless them and their wedding bed. He's convinced that the other Athenian couples will be married at the same time as the Duke and that everything will once again be joyful.

Robin interrupts — he can hear the morning lark! Oberon and Titania leave to walk slowly towards the part of the Earth that is now dark and to talk about the night's events.

Theseus and Hippolyta enter with their servants and Egeus. A hunting horn blows. Theseus asks someone to find the forest ranger so that Hippolyta can hear the sound of the hunting dogs howling. Hippolyta remembers a time, when she was with Hercules and Cadmus, when one of their dogs cornered a bear. The barking, she assures him, was impressive, and echoed off mountains and trees. Theseus suddenly sees the four sleeping Athenians on the ground. Egeus identifies them all. Theseus assumes they came out to the woods knowing that he and Hippolyta would be there. He then realizes that today is the day Hermia is meant to make her decision. Theseus asks the servants to sound the horns to wake them up. They do, and the four wake from their sleep.

They greet Theseus. He asks Lysander and Demetrius if the world is suddenly so peaceful that two enemies can sleep so close to one another. Lysander admits he doesn't truly know how he got there, but the last thing he remembers was his plan to run away with Hermia. Egeus stops him and asks for Theseus to punish him. Demetrius admits that it was true, and he followed them because the beautiful Helena told him where they were going, and was so in love with him that she followed him into the woods. He doesn't quite know how it happened, but his love for Hermia has disappeared, and his love for Helena, who he was once engaged to, has returned. Now, he will always be true to Helena and love her forever.

Theseus overrules Egeus' wishes: the two couples will be married later on after he and Hippolyta are wed. They give up on hunting as the morning grows late, and decide to go back to Athens to get ready for the weddings. All but the four Athenians leave. Demetrius doesn't understand what happened—the previous night's events seem clear and yet cloudy to him. They all agree. Demetrius wonders if they're still asleep and ask them if they saw the Duke, as well. They did. They decide to follow Theseus back to Athens and talk about their dreams along the way. They leave.

Bottom wakes up. He, too, has had a strange "dream". He realizes he has been left alone. He can't put into words what he has just experienced and plans to ask Quince to put it down in words for him as a song. He'll sing it for the Duke during the intermission or when Thisbe dies in the play.

Act Four, Scene Two

Back in Athens, Quince and the others gather to discuss Bottom's whereabouts. They're sure he's been kidnapped as he did not return to his house. They're upset that the play will be ruined now that their lead is nowhere to be found. Snug arrives to tell them that three couples have been married. They're upset about the wages they would have received for putting on the play.

Bottom enters. They're pleased and amazed to see him. He won't tell them about the wondrous dreams he has had just yet as he wants them to get organized for the play. After he gives out several orders, they gather together and leave.

Act Five

Act Five, Scene One

Theseus, Hippolyta, and Philostrate enter. Hippolyta comments that the four Athenians are saying some strange things. Theseus agrees the story sounds perfectly made up, and that he'll never believe them. He blames the hallucinations on love affecting them all. He tells her that when these people are happy, they have such an imagination that they have to blame it on something otherworldly being the cause. Hippolyta points out that they all experienced the same dream, and it remains consistent, so it could perhaps be true.

Demetrius, Helena, Lysander and Hermia arrive. They all wish one another joy in their marriages. Theseus wants to be entertained and asks Philostrate for a list of the entertainment that has been prepared for them while they wait to go to bed. Theseus rejects a few of the plays and performances, either because they are unsuitable, or because he's already heard them. He finally comes to Thisbe and Pyramus, and cannot understand why the play has been pitched as so many contradictory things — both a comedy and a tragedy? Theseus asks for more details. Philostrate tells him the play isn't worth the bother, and the actors are awful. He laughed when he watched the rehearsal of Pyramus' suicide, rather than cried. Theseus wants to see it. Philostrate warns him against it. Theseus will watch it — he's intrigued by ordinary workmen putting on a play, and wants to see what they can do. Philostrate leaves to fetch them.

Hippolyta isn't so sure she'd like to watch poor people making fools of themselves if they can't act, but Theseus assures her that they will be generous with their thanks. Philostrate enters and announces the Prologue is ready to be delivered. Theseus tells him to come in.

Quince as the Prologue warns the audience that they are not there to entertain them, or make them happy. The audience criticizes him for his grammar, speed of delivery and punctuation. The rest of the players come in. Quince continues with the Prologue, and describes the action of the story: Pyramus and Thisbe talk through the chink in the wall and meet by moonlight. A Lion frightens Thisbe, who drops her cloak. The Lion tears through the cloak with his bloodied mouth. Pyramus finds the bloodied cloak and stabs himself in his grief. Thisbe does the same, leaving both of them dead. Quince asks the others to tell the audience more.

Snout tells the audience he is a wall, but no ordinary wall, for his fingers form a chink that the two lovers can talk through. Both Theseus and Demetrius sarcastically praise Snout for his brilliant delivery as they've never heard a wall speak better. Pyramus played by Bottom comes to the wall and is upset that Thisbe has forgotten their meeting time. He curses the wall that separates his and her father's territory. Theseus jokes that the wall should probably talk back. Bottom disagrees. Thisbe finally turns up, and the two lovers talk through the door. After comparing themselves to famous lovers, and trying to kiss one another through the hole in the wall, they decide to meet at Ninny's tomb. Snout leaves, the wall no longer needed in the story. Theseus joke that they should have stuck around for a while longer as the wall no longer separates them. Hippolyta thinks this is the silliest play she's ever seen, but Theseus tells her to use her imagination to fill in the awful spots.

Snug the Lion appears on stage and courteously explains to the audience that he is not a real Lion. The audience compliment him for various characteristics. The Moon then enters, carrying a lantern and explains he represents the Moon. The audience argue whether he represents the Moon well enough. He reveals he is actually playing the man in the Moon, and the lantern represents the Moon itself. None of the audience is sure how exactly the man could fit into the lantern that stands in for the Moon. The Moon gets angry with the audience and tells them that all they need to know is that he is the man in the Moon, the lantern is the Moon, the thorn bush is his thorn bush and the dog, his dog. Demetrius isn't sure how all of these things can fit into the Moon/lantern, but asks them to go on. While Thisbe is frightened by the Lion, and the Lion tears her cloak, the audience compliments them on various elements.

Bottom as Pyramus delivers his emotional lines over the death of Thisbe and then stabs himself. The Moon leaves and Pyramus dies. The audience wonder how Thisbe will find Pyramus without the Moonlight, but they assume the stars and Pyramus' moaning will show her the way. Hippolyta hopes Thisbe won't cry over Pyramus' death too much as he doesn't genuinely deserve it. Thisbe finds Pyramus, stabs herself and dies. The audience joke that the Lion and the Moon will have to bury them. Demetrius adds that the Wall will help too. Bottom breaks character to tell them that the Wall cannot help as it has been taken down. He asks the audience if they would like to hear the Epilogue. Theseus does, not as he doesn't think that a play, which ends with all the characters dead, needs an apology to the audience in at the end as there is no one left to blame. He calls it a good tragedy and asks the actors to dance for them.

As the bell chimes, Theseus announces that it is time for bed, and they should retire to their chambers. They will continue to celebrate for two more weeks, but, for now, they should go to bed. They all leave.

Robin enters. He talks about the kinds of things that happen when night reappears, including the spirits from the graveyards rising up and roaming once more across the land. He's been sent ahead of the fairies to clean up and make sure no one disturbs the sleeping house. Oberon and Titania enter with their fairies. They sing and dance together to bless the house, the marriages, and their future children. They all leave once again except for Robin.

Robin addresses the audience. He tells them that if the play has offended them in any way, that they should think of it like a dream. That nothing they saw actually happened. And if he needs to, he will make things right once again if given a chance. If he doesn't, then he can be called a liar. If they are still friends, they should applaud. He leaves.

The Life and Times of William Shakespeare

The Times Shakespeare Lived In

The Elizabethan London that William Shakespeare arrived in was much different than it is today. Significantly, the population was much smaller. Today, seven and a half million people live in the area known as Greater London. In Shakespeare's time the population was around 200,000 – this still made it an enormous metropolis for the time period and it was the leading city in Europe.

In the sixteenth century London suffered from an extremely high death rate – more people died in the city than were born. It was only the steady influx of newcomers from other English counties and immigrants from Europe that helped London's population grow. The bubonic plague was still a large factor in death counts in the city – in fact many people fled the urban area when the many epidemics rolled through. Shakespeare himself probably returned at times to Stratford when it was healthier to do so. The life expectancy in London at the time was thirty-five years; this seemingly short life expectancy would be lengthened if one survived childhood – many children did not make it to their fifth birthday.

London was a crowded and dirty place – it is not surprising that disease was rampant. The houses were built close together and the streets were very narrow – in many cases only wide enough for a single cart to navigate. There was no indoor plumbing and it would be another three hundred years before a sanitary way of disposing of sewage was built for the city of London.

Shakespeare was born into a time of religious upheaval. The Catholic Church came under pressure from the second Tudor ruler, Henry VIII, to annual his first marriage to Catherine of Aragon. Upon the death of his brother Arthur and Henry's ascendancy to the heir to the English throne, he had married his brother's widow in 1509. Over the years Catherine had given birth to only one surviving heir – a daughter Mary. Twenty-four years later, Henry asked for a divorce so he could marry the young Anne Boleyn. The Pope refused and in 1534 Henry broke from the Church, establishing the Church of England. The throne went to Henry's son Edward VI in 1547 but upon the boy's death in 1553, his half-sister Mary, daughter of Henry and Catherine, became Queen. She was a devout Catholic, and plunged the country back into a period of dissension and conflict, which included persecution and death for Protestants and the re-establishment of the Roman Catholic Church.

Queen Mary's death changed the religious *status quo* in England once again when Queen Elizabeth I came to the throne in 1558. The Catholic Church was once again banned, and the Church of England resurrected in its stead.

England also faced a turning point in its very political existence during Shakespeare's "lost years", those years before his arrival in London when his little is known about his life. In 1588, after Elizabeth I had condemned her cousin Mary, Queen of Scots, to death for conspiracy Spain decided to attack Britain in retaliation for the Roman Catholic Mary's death. The Catholic powers were increasingly fearful of the Protestant movement and with England's break from the Church of Rome now seemingly the final stroke in their relationship, it looked as though Catholicism itself was under threat. Spain rose of fleet of ships to sail upon England and it was thought to be unbeatable. However several factors led to English victory – strategic mistakes on the Spanish side and poor weather were among them. England emerged triumphant, its confidence strong, and the Church of England firmly entrenched. Queen Elizabeth I, known as "Gloriana" always serves as a backdrop to any story of Shakespeare's life. An interesting development during her reign was the acceleration of literacy in Elizabethan England – by the end of her reign, it stood at 33% (probably for males only) and was one of the highest rates in the world.

Queen Elizabeth's reign ended in 1603, when she died in her sleep at the age of sixty-nine. Her cousin's son, James I of Scotland became England's king. He was devoutly Protestant so there was no change in the official Church, and indeed by the beginning of the 17th century, few English citizens had ever attended a Catholic mass.

James enthusiastically supported drama and in particular, Shakespeare's company. Over the next thirteen years, before William's death, the playwright's company would perform for the King one hundred and eighty seven times. It was the time of Shakepeare's greatest dramatic output.

Much information on the London theatres of the day has been gleaned from the journal and business papers of Philip Henslowe, who owned the Rose and Fortune theatres. For his papers we can extrapolate what life for actors and playwrights would have been like during Shakespeare's time. We also know something of the Fortune Theatre's building – the contract to build it has survived. These records were used to build the copy of the Globe Theatre that stands on the banks of the Thames River today. Other information has come from existing diaries and letters that survived the time – mostly from visitors to the city who found the whole experience interesting enough to record.

Shakepeare's Family

William Shakespeare, the son of John Shakespeare and Mary, née Arden, was born in the village of Stratford-upon-Avon in the English county of Warwickshire. Stratford is northwest of London, situated somewhat south of England's center. Shakespeare was born quite possibly on 23 Apr in 1564 – his baptism in the family's parish church on April 26 suggests this. Children in that day and age were often baptized on the third day after their birth.

William was John and Mary's third known child – and the first to survive infancy. His two older sisters, Joan and Margaret, both died before he was born. Of the five younger children (Gilbert, a second Joan, Anne, Richard, and Edmund) Anne died at the age of eight but William's other siblings lived into adulthood. Only the second Joan was to reach what we would consider a good old age – she died in 1646 at the age of seventy-seven.

William's background on his paternal side was, like most of the English of his day, humble. Earlier relatives were not gentry in the least but simple tenant farmers who worked in the parish of nearby Arden. The meaning of the name Shakespeare has long been shrouded in mystery – the rarity of the surname indicates that it probably originated with one man several hundred years before William's birth. Evidence shows that the first Shakespeare was born somewhere north of Warwickshire. By 1389 an Adam Shakespeare was a tenant farmer at Baddesley Clinton in Warwickshire – unfortunately early parish records were not compelled to be kept until not long before William's time so it is not known for sure if he was a direct ancestor. In 1596 William's father John applied for a family coat of arms, citing that his grandfather had been granted land in northern Warwickshire for service under Henry VII in the War of the Roses. Historians believe this was probably a valid claim, but no records have come to light that prove it.

William was the grandson of Richard Shakespeare, a tenant farmer at Snitterfield in Arden who was not a wealthy man but did leave a will in which he named John Shakespeare as administrator, which would indicate he was the eldest surviving son. By the time of Richard's death in 1560, John had been living at nearby Stratford-upon-Avon since 1550. Records show that John had his first house in Henley Street in Stratford by 1552 and had acquired the house next door and one in Greenhill Street by 1556. John's trade was that of a glove-maker and he also worked as a wool dealer and an animal skin-cutter. He may have also worked as a butcher - it would seem that he was a man who was not afraid of work and had some ambition to better himself.

Around 1557 John Shakespeare married Mary Arden, the daughter of the owner of the Snitterfield estate where his father Richard Shakespeare farmed. Mary was the youngest of the eight daughters of Robert Arden – apparently Robert had a hand in marrying his daughters off and John must have seemed a likely prospect at the time – certainly on the social scale the Ardens would have been higher than the Shakespeares.

On his mother's side at least, William's roots in the area were deep. Just to the north of the River Avon is the village of Arden, from which Mary's family undoubtedly took their name. Surnames were beginning to be "set" about four hundred years before William's birth; it is probable that that branch of the family had been in the area for at least that long. William's grandfather Robert Arden was a man of some means, at least locally. He owned several estates, including the one where Richard Shakespeare was a tenant farmer. The Ardens were Roman Catholic – England at the time was seesawing between the old Catholic Church and Protestantism. Although the marriage is not found in a surviving record, it is likely that it took place at Aston Cantlow where Mary's father had been buried in 1556 and the ceremony would have been a Catholic one, as Mary Tudor, who had brought Catholicism back to England as the official church, was on the throne. Not long before William's birth in 1564 Elizabeth I became Queen of England and the country made the final break with Roman Catholicism, and the local parish church became part of the new Church of England.

Shakespeare's Childhood and Education

William Shakespeare's accepted birth date of April 23, 1564 has long been open to dispute, but the month and year are probably correct. There are two reasons April 23rd is the sentimental favorite: it is St. George's Day in England (George is the country's patron saint) and Shakespeare died on the same date fifty-two years later. Baby William was baptized on the 26th of April in the parish church of Stratford-upon-Avon and as infants in Tudor times were traditionally baptized on the third day following their birth, historians have happily settled on the 23rd as his date of birth.

William was the third of eight known children born to John Shakespeare and Mary (Arden) Shakespeare, and the first to survive infancy. In fact young William's first year was overshadowed by the spectre of the Black Death, now known more prosaically as the bubonic plague. About 10% of the residents of Stratford died that year and the Shakespeares' must have felt relief their young family's survival. The plague was to continue to be a problem for England's citizens during the Elizabethan era. William was to lose his younger sister, eight-year-old Anne, to the disease. Quite possibly his older sister Margaret, a one-year-old baby, died of the Black Death as well, as it swept through the area in 1563. The survival of William, as the first born son, and after the deaths of older sisters Joan and Margaret, no doubt gave him a special place in the Shakespeare family.

William's childhood home, in Henley Street, Stratford, is still standing and is a typical Tudor structure with decorative half timber and small windows. In Shakespeare's time the house would have had a thatched roof. Henley Street led out of town and William apparently spent much time as a boy wandering and playing the countryside near at hand. He undoubtedly spoke the local dialect and though his own speech was probably more refined due to his education - and undoubtedly influenced by his mother, who came from a higher social stratum than the Shakespeares - William retained a good "ear" for dialectic speech which is evident in his plays and apparently retained his Warwickshire accent until his death.

William's life as a youngster was rural. His father was a craftsman and a tradesman - a glover and maker of leather goods - and records show that neighbors included a tailor and a haberdasher. But also nearby was a blacksmith - who's trade in those times would have been mostly horses - and shepherds lived nearby. As William rambled around the countryside he would have come into contact with the rural inhabitants of various occupations and he would have been well versed in the area's flora and fauna. It is very likely that he knew all the local fairy stories and tales of ghosts, witches, and hobgoblins, which England's rural denizens of the era were particularly fond of these stories. William's later writings show that he was well acquainted with the terms and practices of the rural pursuits of hunting and fishing - like most of his male contemporaries of the time, the young William probably spent many a happy hour engaged in these activities.

As the son of an alderman, William was entitled to a free education. His father John had become an alderman when William was just a baby – John was appointed to replace another alderman who got himself into trouble with the town council. By 1568 he was elected as an alderman and three years later was chief alderman and deputy to the local bailiff (the town's top magistrate). John was involved in local politics for many years, and although his fortunes and position faltered in later years, his son William was guaranteed the best education Stratford could offer.

William's learning took place at King's New School – which is still operating as a boy's school today. The school was originally granted a charter in 1553 by the learned young King Edward VI – a number of schools were erected in his name. It is thought the school was the last of the King Edward Schools as the adolescent Edward died only nine days after its charter was granted. It was familiarly known as the King's New School, and sometimes shortened even more to New School. Today it is known as King Edward VI School (or K.E.S.) and while no records exist from Shakespeare's time, it is generally accepted that William was a pupil and would have begun his education there around 1570 about the time he turned six years old.

The average school day for the middle class boys of Stratford was not an easy one. Students arrived early in the morning, not long after dawn, and remained in school until 5 PM. Breaks were given for meals. The boys also attended school on Saturdays. Church attendance was part of the school day, and much time was given over to the learning of the classical languages and translating classical texts. The Roman poet Ovid made a strong impression on young William. Classical mythology is evident in William's later works and no doubt their influence can be traced back to those formative days in Stratford's New School.

William probably left school around the age of fifteen. What he did then has not been documented but in the normal course of things, he would have worked for his father, at least for a time. He may have also been a school master – his facility with words and his sharp intellect would have made him a good candidate – but perhaps it was simply not his avocation and as time would prove, writing was. Within a few years, though, William was married. Marriage at eighteen in those days was relatively rare – physical maturation coming later to the young of that era compared to today. William, however, had been courting an older woman, and as nature took its course, Anne Hathaway became pregnant. Pregnant brides were common among the rural population – in fact many believed that fertility should be proven before heading for the altar! William Shakespeare and Anne Hathaway were married by license and as William was under twenty-one, he had to obtain his father's consent to marry. The actual parish where their wedding ceremony took place is not known, though it may have been in Shottery, Anne's home parish.

Shakepeare's Adulthood

By the time William Shakespeare was twenty-one years old, he had become the father of three children. His wife Anne gave birth to daughter Susanna in May 1583 and to twins Judith and Hamnet early in 1785. William does appear in an existing legal record for Stratford concerning property owned by his parents in 1786. Unfortunately very little else is on record for the years before he appears in London.
William most likely remained in Stratford for the first few years of his marriage and his knowledge of leather indicates that he probably worked with his glove-making father after he left school. The story that he had been a school master or tutor has long been conjectured. A story of William teaching in a more the Catholic-friendly county of Lancashire has been bandied about. None of the stories have any real evidence to back them up, however.

William and Anne lived in the house on Henley Street with his parents. It is hard to conceive that he would have deserted his wife and children when the latter were so young – William came from a comfortable solidly middle class family and he would have likely been taught to fulfill his responsibilities. Shakespeare may have spent his working career in London, and hints of philandering came forth, but he always remained faithful to Stratford and returned often and in middle age, he returned for good. How happy or unhappy he and Anne were together is simply not known. The fact that no children were born to Anne after the twins arrived may speak volumes – but it may also simply be that the birth of twins rendered her unable to have more children. That William did send home much of his acquired wealth in London does at least indicate that he had not entirely deserted his family responsibilities – but whether it was done out of love or duty, we do not have any way of knowing. The years between 1585 and 1592 are considered Shakespeare's "lost years". Simply put, there is no hard evidence of what William was doing during those years. We also know little about William's wife Anne – she was one of seven children of Richard Hathaway, a yeoman farmer. She was left a small sum of money in his will when he died the year before her marriage and she was to come into this inheritance upon her marriage. The house she grew up in, known as Anne Hathaway's Cottage, is now open to the public, but is more than a mere cottage, having twelve rooms. It is about a mile from the center of Stratford. Anne's gravestone is still in existence as well, and from it her approximate date of birth is calculated – it records that she died in 1623, aged sixty-seven. No verified portraits of her exist and there is no known written description of what she looked like. Some Shakespearean experts believe that Sonnet 145 was written for Anne – the sonnet only really makes sense when the reader understands the wordplay with "hate" and "away" – close enough to mimic her surname, Hathaway.

What were William's influences before he arrived in London to make his way in the world of drama? Certainly he had enjoyed a classical education as a lad and some historians that theorized that he was somehow exposed to more in his late teens and twenties – even if only as a schoolmaster. As for the world of the stage, despite Shakespeare living in a somewhat isolated and rural area, it was quite common for bands of actors to be traveling the countryside plying their trade. These plague haunted years drove many people out of London and into the healthier countryside and actors had to make a living too. They were not above staging performances wherever they could gather enough people to pay the entrance fee. Actors were usually required to have a patron and many wore a badge that identified him as such – this kept the local authorities from looking upon actors as a liability to their parishes. The companies were often sponsored by men of means and even by the nobility. The first acting company created in the reign of Queen Elizabeth I (who came to the throne in 1558) was Lord Leicester's Men in 1574 – the Earls of Sussex and Oxford also had companies by 1582. There was rivalry between the companies and apparently, the Lord Mayor of London disliked the acting groups intensely. Unfortunately, few records for the acting companies have survived.

At least one acting company, The Queen's Men, put in more than one appearance at Stratford in 1589 – and if William was still living there, he very well could have attended their performances. Again, precisely why Shakespeare went to London is not known – but he may have simply been seduced by the theatre life and combined with his love of words it would have seemed the perfect home for him. Again, conjecture comes into deciding Shakespeare's life (one theory has it that William had clung to the old Catholic ways and went to northern England where there was more toleration) but his reasons for going to London remain a mystery. Fortunately for the literary world, he *was* drawn to the theatre and left a stunning literary legacy.

What did William do once he reached London? Again, we don't know for sure, as there are few employment records that have survived from centuries past. Shakespeare did appear in the London in the late 1580's and if he was immediately attracted to the theatre, he would have headed to Southwark, on the south side of the Thames, where many of the restrictions of the city of London did not apply. The entertainment industry of its day was free to do as they wanted there. A tradition has survived down through the centuries that William first got a job holding horses outside the theatre and then moved up to be a prompter's assistant. It is known that within a few years William was "becoming Shakespeare" and was writing.

With so many blanks to fill in his life and so very little solid evidence of Shakespeare's very existence at this point, how is it known that he was writing by 1592? It is thanks to one Robert Greene, another London writer. Greene published an attack on William, accusing him of plagiarism and calling him an "upstart crow". Greene parodied some lines from the history play *Henry VI Part III* and intimated that Shakespeare was stealing from his competition. Greene died soon after this, but the publisher of the attack apologized in print – which indicates that William, still a young man at twenty-eight, had enough of a reputation or at least enough gall, to demand a retraction.

If *Henry VI Part III* had already been written by 1592, there is a good chance that Parts I and II had already been penned as well. This accomplishment would have been remarkable for such a young man, and one who had not attended university as well. His lack of higher education seemed to be an issue with some of his contemporary writers – snobbism not being exclusive to the modern world. Fellow writers, who looked at Shakespeare critically and no doubt enviously, included Christopher Marlowe and Thomas Nashe.

Henry VI Part III was not William's first play. *The Two Gentlemen of Verona* was written sometime between 1588 and 1590. Although it is difficult to determine exactly when many of his early plays were written, it is thought that *A Comedy of Errors* might have been his first comedic play and could have been written as early as 1591. In 1594, Shakespeare created Titus Andronicus, his first attempt at tragedy.

There is nothing in the scant surviving records to suggest that William worked for a theatrical company during his early years in London. It is very likely he worked as a freelance writer, as many of contemporaries of the time did. Looking again at his private life, it is possible that during his early years he was returning home to Stratford at regular intervals.

It is thought that during his early years, he worked with other writers to produce collaborative works. *Sir Thomas More*, a historical play about the martyred Thomas More who was executed by Henry VIII, was co-written with Anthony Munday and Henry Chettle, the latter being the very publisher who retracted Robert Greene's accusation of plagiarism in 1592. Experts believe this was written during Shakespeare's early period.

It is known that it didn't take long for William's work to attract the interest of several different theatrical companies. *Titus Andronicus* was first performed by Sussex's Men. Pembroke's Men also performed several of William's plays and at least two known performance venues are on record – The Inns of Court and the Bankside Rose playhouse. Some Shakespearean historians believe that William had joined the Queen's Men on tour before he arrived in London – some of his later plays are similar to plays they performed in the mid 1580's.

The theatres of London were not a stable entity in the 1590's. Once again, the pall of the plague hung over the city in the summer of 1592. The Puritans, a Protestant faction that had gained some power in the Elizabethan era, despised what they saw as the licentiousness of theatre life and pressured the city to shut down acting venues in London and Southwark. They blamed the theatres for spreading the Plague. The theatres remained closed for two years.

Whether William remained in London for the duration of the Plague years is unknown, but it is known that he turned to writing poetry. In 1593 the rather racy poem *Venus and Adonis* appeared and was dedicated to Henry Wriothesley, the Earl of Southampton. The Earl was a patron of the arts – he supported several poets and often attended the theatre. Shakespeare may have looked upon him as opportunity knocking; after all, having a patron was easier that freelancing. It has been conjectured that Shakespeare's poems were written to Wriothesley as expressions of love and passion; many have conjectured that Shakespeare had homosexual or bisexual leanings. This could be or it might just be that Shakespeare saw an opportunity and wrote what Wriothesley wanted. Without solid evidence, it is impossible to know.

Shakespeare also dedicated the more serious and tragic poem *The Rape of Lucrece* to Wriothesley in 1594. It was about a Roman married woman who is raped by a Roman prince – she then commits suicide. The Rape of Lucrece was not quite as successful as Venus and Adonis but by now Shakespeare's reputation as a writer was established.

William returned to play writing once the Plague had died down again by the fall of 1594. A new theatrical company was formed by Lord Hunsdon (who was Queen Elizabeth's Lord Chamberlain), and called the Chamberlain's Men. Evidence has survived that indicate that Shakespeare was part of the company. Richard Burbage was also part of Chamberlain's Men – he became the company's star actor and would be the lead in many of the Shakespeare plays that they performed. Many of the actors who belonged to the company also had a financial stake in it.

The Chamberlain's Men did well from the start. They first performed for theatre-owner Philip Henslowe in 1594 and were on the bill at Court later that year over the Christmas season. The Chamberlain's Men main rival in London's theatre world was the Admiral's Men and between the two of them, they put on all theatrical performances in the city. Lord Chamberlain's Men now had a base at the Shoreditch Theatre on the London side of the Thames River. This was an important factor for the rest of William's career – it now settled down to something of permanence. Shakespeare was an asset to the company – he brought in his body of work that could serve as part of the company's repertoire for years to come. William produced about two plays a year until he left London to live out his final days in Stratford.

The first Shakespeare play that was a success after the Plague years was *Richard III*, another history play that chronicled the downfall of the Plantagenet royal house and opened the door for the rise of the Tudor dynasty. No doubt this play was popularly supported by the monarch and her Court of the time. Three other well-regarded and often performed plays were thought to have been written during William's first years with the Chamberlain's Men – *A Midsummer Night's Dream, Romeo and Juliet, Love's Labour Lost,* and *Richard II*. The variety of comedy, tragedy, and history plays reflect Shakespeare's talent and versatility. Around this time Shakespeare garnered high praise from a fellow writer Francis Meres. Meres made reference to William's sonnets, which were not actually published for another eleven years.

Tragedy struck the Shakespeare family in 1596 when William and Anne's only son Hamnet.   In 1597 William, obviously enjoying some material success with his writing career, purchased a larger house in Stratford, New Place, the second largest estate in the parish. Shakespeare still spent much of his time in London but as the years went on, he returned to Stratford more and more. The playwright was not only a creative type – he had a keen business sense, as well, or possibly good advisors.   He invested in property, and by 1599 he was part owner of the Globe Theatre, forever afterward associated with Shakespeare.

After the Globe Theatre was built in 1599 Shakespeare became a prominent member of the King's Men – the company was sponsored by the King himself, James I, when he ascended the throne in 1603. The company was commanded to produce and perform plays "for our (the King's) solace and pleasure". Shakespeare produced a great body of work over the next ten years. The Globe burned down during a performance of Henry VIII (a fired canon caused the thatched roof to catch fire). No one was killed, and the Globe was rebuilt soon after. At about this time, after investing in the new theatre, Shakespeare retired to spend most of his time in Stratford. He died at New Place on his 52nd birthday. He was survived by his wife, two daughters, two sons-in-law, and a grandchild. His wife Anne outlived him, dying in 1623. One of the few official documentation of Shakepeare's to have survived is his will – in which he left his wife "his second-best bed" (by law, she would have also inherited one-third of his estate). William and Anne were survived by their two daughters, both married and who would leave descendants.

Play

Characters

THESEUS, Duke of Athens.

EGEUS, Father to Hermia.

LYSANDER, in love with Hermia.

DEMETRIUS, in love with Hermia.

PHILOSTRATE, Master of the Revels to Theseus.

QUINCE, the Carpenter.

SNUG, the Joiner.

BOTTOM, the Weaver.

FLUTE, the Bellows-mender.

SNOUT, the Tinker.

STARVELING, the Tailor.

HIPPOLYTA, Queen of the Amazons, bethrothed to Theseus.

HERMIA, daughter to Egeus, in love with Lysander.

HELENA, in love with Demetrius.

OBERON, King of the Fairies.

TITANIA, Queen of the Fairies.

PUCK, or ROBIN GOODFELLOW, a Fairy.

PEASBLOSSOM, Fairy.

COBWEB, Fairy.

MOTH, Fairy.

MUSTARDSEED, Fairy.

PYRAMUS, THISBE, WALL, MOONSHINE, LION,
Characters in the Interlude performed by the Clowns.

Other Fairies attending their King and Queen. Attendants on
Theseus and Hippolyta.

Act I

Scene I

Athens. A room in the Palace of THESEUS.

[Enter THESEUS, HIPPOLYTA, PHILOSTRATE, and Attendants.]

THESEUS Now, fair Hippolyta, our nuptial hour Draws on apace; four happy days bring in Another moon; but, oh, methinks, how slow This old moon wanes! she lingers my desires, Like to a step-dame or a dowager, Long withering out a young man's revenue.

HIPPOLYTA Four days will quickly steep themselves in nights; Four nights will quickly dream away the time; And then the moon, like to a silver bow New bent in heaven, shall behold the night Of our solemnities.

THESEUS Go, Philostrate, Stir up the Athenian youth to merriments; Awake the pert and nimble spirit of mirth; Turn melancholy forth to funerals-- The pale companion is not for our pomp. --

[Exit PHILOSTRATE.]

Hippolyta, I woo'd thee with my sword, And won thy love doing thee injuries; But I will wed thee in another key, With pomp, with triumph, and with revelling.

[Enter EGEUS, HERMIA, LYSANDER, and DEMETRIUS.]

EGEUS Happy be Theseus, our renowned duke!

THESEUS Thanks, good Egeus: what's the news with thee?

EGEUS Full of vexation come I, with complaint Against my child, my daughter Hermia.-- Stand forth, Demetrius.--My noble lord, This man hath my consent to marry her:-- Stand forth, Lysander;--and, my gracious duke, This man hath bewitch'd the bosom of my child. Thou, thou, Lysander, thou hast given her rhymes, And interchang'd love-tokens with my child: Thou hast by moonlight at her window sung, With feigning voice, verses of feigning love; And stol'n the impression of her fantasy With bracelets of thy hair, rings, gawds, conceits, Knacks, trifles, nosegays, sweetmeats,-- messengers Of strong prevailment in unharden'd youth;-- With cunning hast thou filch'd my daughter's heart; Turned her obedience, which is due to me, To stubborn harshness.-- And, my gracious duke, Be it so she will not here before your grace Consent to marry with Demetrius, I beg the ancient privilege of Athens,-- As she is mine I may dispose of her: Which shall be either to this gentleman Or to her death; according to our law Immediately provided in that case.

THESEUS What say you, Hermia? be advis'd, fair maid: To you your father should be as a god; One that compos'd your beauties: yea, and one To whom you are but as a form in wax, By him imprinted, and within his power To leave the figure, or disfigure it. Demetrius is a worthy gentleman.

HERMIA So is Lysander.

THESEUS In himself he is: But, in this kind, wanting your father's voice, The other must be held the worthier.

HERMIA I would my father look'd but with my eyes.

THESEUS Rather your eyes must with his judgment look.

HERMIA I do entreat your grace to pardon me. I know not by what power I am made bold, Nor how it may concern my modesty In such a presence here to plead my thoughts: But I beseech your grace that I may know The worst that may befall me in this case If I refuse to wed Demetrius.

THESEUS Either to die the death, or to abjure For ever the society of men. Therefore, fair Hermia, question your desires, Know of your youth, examine well your blood, Whether, if you yield not to your father's choice, You can endure the livery of a nun; For aye to be shady cloister mew'd, To live a barren sister all your life, Chanting faint hymns to the cold, fruitless moon. Thrice-blessed they that master so their blood To undergo such maiden pilgrimage: But earthlier happy is the rose distill'd Than that which, withering on the virgin thorn, Grows, lives, and dies, in single blessedness.

HERMIA So will I grow, so live, so die, my lord, Ere I will yield my virgin patent up Unto his lordship, whose unwished yoke My soul consents not to give sovereignty.

THESEUS Take time to pause; and by the next new moon,-- The sealing-day betwixt my love and me For everlasting bond of fellowship,-- Upon that day either prepare to die For disobedience to your father's will; Or else to wed Demetrius, as he would; Or on Diana's altar to protest For aye austerity and single life.

DEMETRIUS Relent, sweet Hermia;--and, Lysander, yield Thy crazed title to my certain right.

LYSANDER You have her father's love, Demetrius; Let me have Hermia's: do you marry him.

EGEUS Scornful Lysander! true, he hath my love; And what is mine my love shall render him; And she is mine; and all my right of her I do estate unto Demetrius.

LYSANDER I am, my lord, as well deriv'd as he, As well possess'd; my love is more than his; My fortunes every way as fairly rank'd, If not with vantage, as Demetrius's; And, which is more than all these boasts can be, I am belov'd of beauteous Hermia: Why should not I then prosecute my right? Demetrius, I'll avouch it to his head, Made love to Nedar's daughter, Helena, And won her soul; and she, sweet lady, dotes, Devoutly dotes, dotes in idolatry, Upon this spotted and inconstant man.

THESEUS I must confess that I have heard so much, And with Demetrius thought to have spoke thereof; But, being over-full of self-affairs, My mind did lose it.--But, Demetrius, come; And come, Egeus; you shall go with me; I have some private schooling for you both.-- For you, fair Hermia, look you arm yourself To fit your fancies to your father's will, Or else the law of Athens yields you up,-- Which by no means we may extenuate,-- To death, or to a vow of single life.-- Come, my Hippolyta: what cheer, my love? Demetrius, and Egeus, go along; I must employ you in some business Against our nuptial, and confer with you Of something nearly that concerns yourselves.

EGEUS With duty and desire we follow you.

[Exeunt THESEUS, HIPPOLYTA, EGEUS, DEMETRIUS, and Train.]

LYSANDER How now, my love! why is your cheek so pale? How chance the roses there do fade so fast?

HERMIA Belike for want of rain, which I could well Beteem them from the tempest of my eyes.

LYSANDER Ah me! for aught that I could ever read, Could ever hear by tale or history, The course of true love never did run smooth: But either it was different in blood,--

HERMIA O cross! Too high to be enthrall'd to low!

LYSANDER Or else misgraffed in respect of years;--

HERMIA O spite! Too old to be engag'd to young!

LYSANDER Or else it stood upon the choice of friends:

HERMIA O hell! to choose love by another's eye!

LYSANDER Or, if there were a sympathy in choice, War, death, or sickness, did lay siege to it, Making it momentary as a sound, Swift as a shadow, short as any dream; Brief as the lightning in the collied night That, in a spleen, unfolds both heaven and earth, And ere a man hath power to say, Behold! The jaws of darkness do devour it up: So quick bright things come to confusion.

HERMIA If then true lovers have ever cross'd, It stands as an edict in destiny: Then let us teach our trial patience, Because it is a customary cross; As due to love as thoughts, and dreams, and sighs, Wishes and tears, poor fancy's followers.

LYSANDER A good persuasion; therefore, hear me, Hermia. I have a widow aunt, a dowager Of great revenue, and she hath no child: From Athens is her house remote seven leagues; And she respects me as her only son. There, gentle Hermia, may I marry thee; And to that place the sharp Athenian law Cannot pursue us. If thou lovest me then, Steal forth thy father's house tomorrow night; And in the wood, a league without the town, Where I did meet thee once with Helena, To do observance to a morn of May, There will I stay for thee.

HERMIA My good Lysander! I swear to thee by Cupid's strongest bow, By his best arrow, with the golden head, By the simplicity of Venus' doves, By that which knitteth souls and prospers loves, And by that fire which burn'd the Carthage queen, When the false Trojan under sail was seen,-- By all the vows that ever men have broke, In number more than ever women spoke,-- In that same place thou hast appointed me, Tomorrow truly will I meet with thee.

LYSANDER Keep promise, love. Look, here comes Helena.

[Enter HELENA.]

HERMIA God speed fair Helena! Whither away?

HELENA Call you me fair? that fair again unsay. Demetrius loves your fair. O happy fair! Your eyes are lode-stars; and your tongue's sweet air More tuneable than lark to shepherd's ear, When wheat is green, when hawthorn buds appear. Sickness is catching: O, were favour so, Yours would I catch, fair Hermia, ere I go; My ear should catch your voice, my eye your eye, My tongue should catch your tongue's sweet melody. Were the world mine, Demetrius being bated, The rest I'd give to be to you translated. O, teach me how you look; and with what art You sway the motion of Demetrius' heart!

HERMIA I frown upon him, yet he loves me still.

HELENA O that your frowns would teach my smiles such skill!

HERMIA I give him curses, yet he gives me love.

HELENA O that my prayers could such affection move!

HERMIA The more I hate, the more he follows me.

HELENA The more I love, the more he hateth me.

HERMIA His folly, Helena, is no fault of mine.

HELENA None, but your beauty: would that fault were mine!

HERMIA Take comfort; he no more shall see my face; Lysander and myself will fly this place.-- Before the time I did Lysander see, Seem'd Athens as a paradise to me: O, then, what graces in my love do dwell, That he hath turn'd a heaven unto hell!

LYSANDER Helen, to you our minds we will unfold: To-morrow night, when Phoebe doth behold Her silver visage in the watery glass, Decking with liquid pearl the bladed grass,-- A time that lovers' flights doth still conceal,-- Through Athens' gates have we devis'd to steal.

HERMIA And in the wood where often you and I Upon faint primrose beds were wont to lie, Emptying our bosoms of their counsel sweet, There my Lysander and myself shall meet: And thence from Athens turn away our eyes, To seek new friends and stranger companies. Farewell, sweet playfellow: pray thou for us, And good luck grant thee thy Demetrius!-- Keep word, Lysander: we must starve our sight From lovers' food, till morrow deep midnight.

LYSANDER I will, my Hermia.

[Exit HERMIA.]

LYSANDER Helena, adieu: As you on him, Demetrius dote on you!

[Exit LYSANDER.]

HELENA How happy some o'er other some can be! Through Athens I am thought as fair as she. But what of that? Demetrius thinks not so; He will not know what all but he do know. And as he errs, doting on Hermia's eyes, So I, admiring of his qualities. Things base and vile, holding no quantity, Love can transpose to form and dignity. Love looks not with the eyes, but with the mind; And therefore is wing'd Cupid painted blind. Nor hath love's mind of any judgment taste; Wings and no eyes figure unheedy haste: And therefore is love said to be a child, Because in choice he is so oft beguil'd. As waggish boys in game themselves forswear, So the boy Love is perjur'd everywhere: For ere Demetrius look'd on Hermia's eyne, He hail'd down oaths that he was only mine; And when this hail some heat from Hermia felt, So he dissolv'd, and showers of oaths did melt. I will go tell him of fair Hermia's flight; Then to the wood will he to-morrow night Pursue her; and for this intelligence If I have thanks, it is a dear expense: But herein mean I to enrich my pain, To have his sight thither and back again.

[Exit HELENA.]

Scene II

The Same. A Room in a Cottage.

[Enter SNUG, BOTTOM, FLUTE, SNOUT, QUINCE, and STARVELING.]

QUINCE Is all our company here?

BOTTOM You were best to call them generally, man by man, according to the scrip.

QUINCE Here is the scroll of every man's name, which is thought fit, through all Athens, to play in our interlude before the duke and duchess on his wedding-day at night.

BOTTOM First, good Peter Quince, say what the play treats on; then read the names of the actors; and so grow to a point.

QUINCE Marry, our play is--The most lamentable comedy and most cruel death of Pyramus and Thisby.

BOTTOM A very good piece of work, I assure you, and a merry.-- Now, good Peter Quince, call forth your actors by the scroll.-- Masters, spread yourselves.

QUINCE Answer, as I call you.--Nick Bottom, the weaver.

BOTTOM Ready. Name what part I am for, and proceed.

QUINCE You, Nick Bottom, are set down for Pyramus.

BOTTOM What is Pyramus? a lover, or a tyrant?

QUINCE A lover, that kills himself most gallantly for love.

BOTTOM That will ask some tears in the true performing of it. If I do it, let the audience look to their eyes; I will move storms; I will condole in some measure. To the rest:--yet my chief humour is for a tyrant: I could play Ercles rarely, or a part to tear a cat in, to make all split.

The raging rocks And shivering shocks Shall break the locks Of prison gates:

And Phibbus' car Shall shine from far, And make and mar The foolish Fates.

This was lofty.--Now name the rest of the players.--This is Ercles' vein, a tyrant's vein;--a lover is more condoling.

QUINCE Francis Flute, the bellows-mender.

FLUTE Here, Peter Quince.

QUINCE Flute, you must take Thisby on you.

FLUTE What is Thisby? a wandering knight?

QUINCE It is the lady that Pyramus must love.

FLUTE Nay, faith, let not me play a woman; I have a beard coming.

QUINCE That's all one; you shall play it in a mask, and you may speak as small as you will.

BOTTOM An I may hide my face, let me play Thisby too: I'll speak in a monstrous little voice;--'Thisne, Thisne!'-- 'Ah, Pyramus, my lover dear; thy Thisby dear! and lady dear!'

QUINCE No, no, you must play Pyramus; and, Flute, you Thisby.

BOTTOM Well, proceed.

QUINCE Robin Starveling, the tailor.

STARVELING Here, Peter Quince.

QUINCE Robin Starveling, you must play Thisby's mother.--Tom Snout, the tinker.

SNOUT Here, Peter Quince.

QUINCE You, Pyramus' father; myself, Thisby's father;--Snug, the joiner, you, the lion's part:--and, I hope, here is a play fitted.

SNUG Have you the lion's part written? pray you, if it be, give it me, for I am slow of study.

QUINCE You may do it extempore, for it is nothing but roaring.

BOTTOM Let me play the lion too: I will roar that I will do any man's heart good to hear me; I will roar that I will make the duke say 'Let him roar again, let him roar again.'

QUINCE An you should do it too terribly, you would fright the duchess and the ladies, that they would shriek; and that were enough to hang us all.

ALL That would hang us every mother's son.

BOTTOM I grant you, friends, if you should fright the ladies out of their wits, they would have no more discretion but to hang us: but I will aggravate my voice so, that I will roar you as gently as any sucking dove; I will roar you an 'twere any nightingale.

QUINCE You can play no part but Pyramus; for Pyramus is a sweet-faced man; a proper man, as one shall see in a summer's day; a most lovely gentleman-like man; therefore you must needs play Pyramus.

BOTTOM Well, I will undertake it. What beard were I best to play it in?

QUINCE Why, what you will.

BOTTOM I will discharge it in either your straw-colour beard, your orange-tawny beard, your purple-in-grain beard, or your French-crown-colour beard, your perfect yellow.

QUINCE Some of your French crowns have no hair at all, and then you will play bare-faced.-- But, masters, here are your parts: and I am to entreat you, request you, and desire you, to con them by to-morrow night; and meet me in the palace wood, a mile without the town, by moonlight; there will we rehearse: for if we meet in the city, we shall be dogg'd with company, and our devices known. In the meantime I will draw a bill of properties, such as our play wants. I pray you, fail me not.

BOTTOM We will meet; and there we may rehearse most obScenely and courageously. Take pains; be perfect; adieu.

QUINCE At the duke's oak we meet.

BOTTOM Enough; hold, or cut bow-strings.

[Exeunt.]

Act II

Scene I

A wood near Athens.

[Enter a FAIRY at One door, and PUCK at another.]

PUCK How now, spirit! whither wander you?

FAIRY Over hill, over dale, Thorough bush, thorough brier, Over park, over pale, Thorough flood, thorough fire, I do wander everywhere, Swifter than the moon's sphere; And I serve the fairy queen, To dew her orbs upon the green. The cowslips tall her pensioners be: In their gold coats spots you see; Those be rubies, fairy favours, In those freckles live their savours; I must go seek some dew-drops here, And hang a pearl in every cowslip's ear. Farewell, thou lob of spirits; I'll be gone: Our queen and all her elves come here anon.

PUCK The king doth keep his revels here to-night; Take heed the Queen come not within his sight. For Oberon is passing fell and wrath, Because that she, as her attendant, hath A lovely boy, stol'n from an Indian king; She never had so sweet a changeling: And jealous Oberon would have the child Knight of his train, to trace the forests wild: But she perforce withholds the loved boy, Crowns him with flowers, and makes him all her joy: And now they never meet in grove or green, By fountain clear, or spangled starlight sheen, But they do square; that all their elves for fear Creep into acorn cups, and hide them there.

FAIRY Either I mistake your shape and making quite, Or else you are that shrewd and knavish sprite Call'd Robin Goodfellow: are not you he That frights the maidens of the villagery; Skim milk, and sometimes labour in the quern, And bootless make the breathless housewife churn; And sometime make the drink to bear no barm; Mislead night-wanderers, laughing at their harm? Those that Hobgoblin call you, and sweet Puck, You do their work, and they shall have good luck: Are not you he?

PUCK Thou speak'st aright; I am that merry wanderer of the night. I jest to Oberon, and make him smile, When I a fat and bean-fed horse beguile, Neighing in likeness of a filly foal; And sometime lurk I in a gossip's bowl, In very likeness of a roasted crab; And, when she drinks, against her lips I bob, And on her withered dewlap pour the ale. The wisest aunt, telling the saddest tale, Sometime for three-foot stool mistaketh me; Then slip I from her bum, down topples she, And 'tailor' cries, and falls into a cough; And then the whole quire hold their hips and loffe, And waxen in their mirth, and neeze, and swear A merrier hour was never wasted there.-- But room, fairy, here comes Oberon.

FAIRY And here my mistress.--Would that he were gone!

[Enter OBERON at one door, with his Train, and TITANIA, at another, with hers.]

OBERON Ill met by moonlight, proud Titania.

TITANIA What, jealous Oberon! Fairies, skip hence; I have forsworn his bed and company.

OBERON Tarry, rash wanton: am not I thy lord?

TITANIA Then I must be thy lady; but I know When thou hast stol'n away from fairy-land, And in the shape of Corin sat all day, Playing on pipes of corn, and versing love To amorous Phillida. Why art thou here, Come from the farthest steep of India, But that, forsooth, the bouncing Amazon, Your buskin'd mistress and your warrior love, To Theseus must be wedded; and you come To give their bed joy and prosperity.

OBERON How canst thou thus, for shame, Titania, Glance at my credit with Hippolyta, Knowing I know thy love to Theseus? Didst not thou lead him through the glimmering night From Perigenia, whom he ravish'd? And make him with fair Aegle break his faith, With Ariadne and Antiopa?

TITANIA These are the forgeries of jealousy: And never, since the middle summer's spring, Met we on hill, in dale, forest, or mead, By paved fountain, or by rushy brook, Or on the beached margent of the sea, To dance our ringlets to the whistling wind, But with thy brawls thou hast disturb'd our sport. Therefore the winds, piping to us in vain, As in revenge, have suck'd up from the sea Contagious fogs; which, falling in the land, Hath every pelting river made so proud That they have overborne their continents: The ox hath therefore stretch'd his yoke in vain, The ploughman lost his sweat; and the green corn Hath rotted ere his youth attain'd a beard: The fold stands empty in the drowned field, And crows are fatted with the murrion flock; The nine men's morris is fill'd up with mud; And the quaint mazes in the wanton green, For lack of tread, are undistinguishable: The human mortals want their winter here; No night is now with hymn or carol blest:-- Therefore the moon, the governess of floods, Pale in her anger, washes all the air, That rheumatic diseases do abound: And thorough this distemperature we see The seasons alter: hoary-headed frosts Fall in the fresh lap of the crimson rose; And on old Hyem's thin and icy crown An odorous chaplet of sweet summer buds Is, as in mockery, set: the spring, the summer, The childing autumn, angry winter, change Their wonted liveries; and the maz'd world, By their increase, now knows not which is which: And this same progeny of evils comes From our debate, from our dissension: We are their parents and original.

OBERON Do you amend it, then: it lies in you: Why should Titania cross her Oberon? I do but beg a little changeling boy To be my henchman.

TITANIA Set your heart at rest; The fairy-land buys not the child of me. His mother was a vot'ress of my order: And, in the spiced Indian air, by night, Full often hath she gossip'd by my side; And sat with me on Neptune's yellow sands, Marking the embarked traders on the flood; When we have laugh'd to see the sails conceive, And grow big-bellied with the wanton wind; Which she, with pretty and with swimming gait Following,--her womb then rich with my young squire,-- Would imitate; and sail upon the land, To fetch me trifles, and return again, As from a voyage, rich with merchandise. But she, being mortal, of that boy did die; And for her sake do I rear up her boy: And for her sake I will not part with him.

OBERON How long within this wood intend you stay?

TITANIA Perchance till after Theseus' wedding-day. If you will patiently dance in our round, And see our moonlight revels, go with us; If not, shun me, and I will spare your haunts.

OBERON Give me that boy and I will go with thee.

TITANIA Not for thy fairy kingdom. Fairies, away: We shall chide downright if I longer stay.

[Exit TITANIA with her Train.]

OBERON Well, go thy way: thou shalt not from this grove Till I torment thee for this injury.-- My gentle Puck, come hither: thou remember'st Since once I sat upon a promontory, And heard a mermaid, on a dolphin's back, Uttering such dulcet and harmonious breath, That the rude sea grew civil at her song, And certain stars shot madly from their spheres To hear the sea-maid's music.

PUCK I remember.

OBERON That very time I saw,--but thou couldst not,-- Flying between the cold moon and the earth, Cupid, all arm'd: a certain aim he took At a fair vestal, throned by the west; And loos'd his love-shaft smartly from his bow, As it should pierce a hundred thousand hearts; But I might see young Cupid's fiery shaft Quench'd in the chaste beams of the watery moon; And the imperial votaress passed on, In maiden meditation, fancy-free. Yet mark'd I where the bolt of Cupid fell: It fell upon a little western flower,-- Before milk-white, now purple with love's wound,-- And maidens call it love-in-idleness. Fetch me that flower, the herb I showed thee once: The juice of it on sleeping eyelids laid Will make or man or woman madly dote Upon the next live creature that it sees. Fetch me this herb: and be thou here again Ere the leviathan can swim a league.

PUCK I'll put a girdle round about the earth In forty minutes.

[Exit PUCK.]

OBERON Having once this juice, I'll watch Titania when she is asleep, And drop the liquor of it in her eyes: The next thing then she waking looks upon,-- Be it on lion, bear, or wolf, or bull, On meddling monkey, or on busy ape,-- She shall pursue it with the soul of love. And ere I take this charm from off her sight,-- As I can take it with another herb, I'll make her render up her page to me. But who comes here? I am invisible; And I will overhear their conference.

[Enter DEMETRIUS, HELENA following him.]

DEMETRIUS I love thee not, therefore pursue me not. Where is Lysander and fair Hermia? The one I'll slay, the other slayeth me. Thou told'st me they were stol'n into this wood, And here am I, and wode within this wood, Because I cannot meet with Hermia. Hence, get thee gone, and follow me no more.

HELENA You draw me, you hard-hearted adamant; But yet you draw not iron, for my heart Is true as steel. Leave you your power to draw, And I shall have no power to follow you.

DEMETRIUS Do I entice you? Do I speak you fair? Or, rather, do I not in plainest truth Tell you I do not, nor I cannot love you?

HELENA And even for that do I love you the more. I am your spaniel; and, Demetrius, The more you beat me, I will fawn on you: Use me but as your spaniel, spurn me, strike me, Neglect me, lose me; only give me leave, Unworthy as I am, to follow you. What worser place can I beg in your love, And yet a place of high respect with me,-- Than to be used as you use your dog?

DEMETRIUS Tempt not too much the hatred of my spirit; For I am sick when I do look on thee.

HELENA And I am sick when I look not on you.

DEMETRIUS You do impeach your modesty too much, To leave the city, and commit yourself Into the hands of one that loves you not; To trust the opportunity of night, And the ill counsel of a desert place, With the rich worth of your virginity.

HELENA Your virtue is my privilege for that. It is not night when I do see your face, Therefore I think I am not in the night; Nor doth this wood lack worlds of company; For you, in my respect, are all the world: Then how can it be said I am alone When all the world is here to look on me?

DEMETRIUS I'll run from thee, and hide me in the brakes, And leave thee to the mercy of wild beasts.

HELENA The wildest hath not such a heart as you. Run when you will, the story shall be chang'd; Apollo flies, and Daphne holds the chase; The dove pursues the griffin; the mild hind Makes speed to catch the tiger,--bootless speed, When cowardice pursues and valour flies.

DEMETRIUS I will not stay thy questions; let me go: Or, if thou follow me, do not believe But I shall do thee mischief in the wood.

HELENA Ay, in the temple, in the town, the field, You do me mischief. Fie, Demetrius! Your wrongs do set a scandal on my sex: We cannot fight for love as men may do: We should be woo'd, and were not made to woo. I'll follow thee, and make a heaven of hell, To die upon the hand I love so well.

[Exeunt DEMETRIUS and HELENA.]

OBERON Fare thee well, nymph: ere he do leave this grove, Thou shalt fly him, and he shall seek thy love.--

[Re-enter PUCK.]

Hast thou the flower there? Welcome, wanderer.

PUCK Ay, there it is.

OBERON I pray thee give it me. I know a bank whereon the wild thyme blows, Where ox-lips and the nodding violet grows; Quite over-canopied with luscious woodbine, With sweet musk-roses, and with eglantine: There sleeps Titania sometime of the night, Lulled in these flowers with dances and delight; And there the snake throws her enamell'd skin, Weed wide enough to wrap a fairy in: And with the juice of this I'll streak her eyes, And make her full of hateful fantasies. Take thou some of it, and seek through this grove: A sweet Athenian lady is in love With a disdainful youth: anoint his eyes; But do it when the next thing he espies May be the lady: thou shalt know the man By the Athenian garments he hath on. Effect it with some care, that he may prove More fond on her than she upon her love: And look thou meet me ere the first cock crow.

PUCK Fear not, my lord; your servant shall do so.

[Exeunt.]

Scene II

Another part of the wood.

[Enter TITANIA, with her Train.]

TITANIA Come, now a roundel and a fairy song; Then, for the third part of a minute, hence; Some to kill cankers in the musk-rose buds; Some war with rere-mice for their leathern wings, To make my small elves coats; and some keep back The clamorous owl, that nightly hoots and wonders At our quaint spirits. Sing me now asleep; Then to your offices, and let me rest.

SONG. I. FIRST FAIRY You spotted snakes, with double tongue, Thorny hedgehogs, be not seen; Newts and blind-worms do no wrong; Come not near our fairy queen:

CHORUS. Philomel, with melody, Sing in our sweet lullaby: Lulla, lulla, lullaby; lulla, lulla, lullaby: Never harm, nor spell, nor charm, Come our lovely lady nigh; So good-night, with lullaby.

II. SECOND FAIRY Weaving spiders, come not here; Hence, you long-legg'd spinners, hence; Beetles black, approach not near; Worm nor snail do no offence.

CHORUS Philomel with melody, &c.

FIRST FAIRY Hence away; now all is well. One, aloof, stand sentinel.

[Exeunt Fairies. TITANIA sleeps.]

[Enter OBERON.]

OBERON What thou seest when thou dost wake, [Squeezes the flower on TITANIA'S eyelids.] Do it for thy true-love take; Love and languish for his sake; Be it ounce, or cat, or bear, Pard, or boar with bristled hair, In thy eye that shall appear When thou wak'st, it is thy dear; Wake when some vile thing is near.

[Exit.]

[Enter LYSANDER and HERMIA.]

LYSANDER Fair love, you faint with wandering in the wood; And, to speak troth, I have forgot our way; We'll rest us, Hermia, if you think it good, And tarry for the comfort of the day.

HERMIA Be it so, Lysander: find you out a bed, For I upon this bank will rest my head.

LYSANDER One turf shall serve as pillow for us both; One heart, one bed, two bosoms, and one troth.

HERMIA Nay, good Lysander; for my sake, my dear, Lie farther off yet, do not lie so near.

LYSANDER O, take the sense, sweet, of my innocence; Love takes the meaning in love's conference. I mean that my heart unto yours is knit; So that but one heart we can make of it: Two bosoms interchained with an oath; So then two bosoms and a single troth. Then by your side no bed-room me deny; For lying so, Hermia, I do not lie.

HERMIA Lysander riddles very prettily:-- Now much beshrew my manners and my pride If Hermia meant to say Lysander lied! But, gentle friend, for love and courtesy Lie further off; in human modesty, Such separation as may well be said Becomes a virtuous bachelor and a maid: So far be distant; and good night, sweet friend: Thy love ne'er alter till thy sweet life end!

LYSANDER Amen, amen, to that fair prayer say I; And then end life when I end loyalty! Here is my bed: Sleep give thee all his rest!

HERMIA With half that wish the wisher's eyes be pressed!

[They sleep.]

[Enter PUCK.]

PUCK Through the forest have I gone, But Athenian found I none, On whose eyes I might approve This flower's force in stirring love. Night and silence! Who is here? Weeds of Athens he doth wear: This is he, my master said, Despised the Athenian maid; And here the maiden, sleeping sound, On the dank and dirty ground. Pretty soul! she durst not lie Near this lack-love, this kill-courtesy. Churl, upon thy eyes I throw All the power this charm doth owe; When thou wak'st let love forbid Sleep his seat on thy eyelid: So awake when I am gone; For I must now to Oberon.

[Exit.]

[Enter DEMETRIUS and HELENA, running.]

HELENA Stay, though thou kill me, sweet Demetrius.

DEMETRIUS I charge thee, hence, and do not haunt me thus.

HELENA O, wilt thou darkling leave me? do not so.

DEMETRIUS. Stay on thy peril; I alone will go.

[Exit DEMETRIUS.]

HELENA O, I am out of breath in this fond chase! The more my prayer, the lesser is my grace. Happy is Hermia, wheresoe'er she lies, For she hath blessed and attractive eyes. How came her eyes so bright? Not with salt tears: If so, my eyes are oftener wash'd than hers. No, no, I am as ugly as a bear; For beasts that meet me run away for fear: Therefore no marvel though Demetrius Do, as a monster, fly my presence thus. What wicked and dissembling glass of mine Made me compare with Hermia's sphery eyne?-- But who is here?-- Lysander! on the ground! Dead? or asleep? I see no blood, no wound. Lysander, if you live, good sir, awake.

LYSANDER [Waking.] And run through fire I will for thy sweet sake. Transparent Helena! Nature shows art, That through thy bosom makes me see thy heart. Where is Demetrius? O, how fit a word Is that vile name to perish on my sword!

HELENA Do not say so, Lysander; say not so: What though he love your Hermia? Lord, what though? Yet Hermia still loves you: then be content.

LYSANDER. Content with Hermia? No: I do repent The tedious minutes I with her have spent. Not Hermia but Helena I love: Who will not change a raven for a dove? The will of man is by his reason sway'd; And reason says you are the worthier maid. Things growing are not ripe until their season; So I, being young, till now ripe not to reason; And touching now the point of human skill, Reason becomes the marshal to my will, And leads me to your eyes, where I o'erlook Love's stories, written in love's richest book.

HELENA Wherefore was I to this keen mockery born? When at your hands did I deserve this scorn? Is't not enough, is't not enough, young man, That I did never, no, nor never can Deserve a sweet look from Demetrius' eye, But you must flout my insufficiency? Good troth, you do me wrong,--good sooth, you do-- In such disdainful manner me to woo. But fare you well: perforce I must confess, I thought you lord of more true gentleness. O, that a lady of one man refus'd Should of another therefore be abus'd!

[Exit.]

LYSANDER She sees not Hermia:--Hermia, sleep thou there; And never mayst thou come Lysander near! For, as a surfeit of the sweetest things The deepest loathing to the stomach brings; Or, as the heresies that men do leave Are hated most of those they did deceive; So thou, my surfeit and my heresy, Of all be hated, but the most of me! And, all my powers, address your love and might To honour Helen, and to be her knight!

[Exit.]

HERMIA [Starting.] Help me, Lysander, help me! do thy best To pluck this crawling serpent from my breast! Ay me, for pity!--What a dream was here! Lysander, look how I do quake with fear! Methought a serpent eat my heart away, And you sat smiling at his cruel prey.-- Lysander! what, removed? Lysander! lord! What, out of hearing? gone? no sound, no word? Alack, where are you? speak, an if you hear; Speak, of all loves! I swoon almost with fear. No?--then I well perceive you are not nigh: Either death or you I'll find immediately.

[Exit.]

Act III

Scene I

The Wood. The Queen of Fairies lying asleep.

[Enter QUINCE, SNUG, BOTTOM, FLUTE, SNOUT, and STARVELING.]

BOTTOM Are we all met?

QUINCE Pat, pat; and here's a marvellous convenient place for our rehearsal. This green plot shall be our stage, this hawthorn brake our tiring-house; and we will do it in action, as we will do it before the duke.

BOTTOM Peter Quince,--

QUINCE What sayest thou, bully Bottom?

BOTTOM There are things in this comedy of 'Pyramus and Thisby' that will never please. First, Pyramus must draw a sword to kill himself; which the ladies cannot abide. How answer you that?

SNOUT By'r lakin, a parlous fear.

STARVELING I believe we must leave the killing out, when all is done.

BOTTOM Not a whit: I have a device to make all well. Write me a prologue; and let the prologue seem to say we will do no harm with our swords, and that Pyramus is not killed indeed; and for the more better assurance, tell them that I Pyramus am not Pyramus but Bottom the weaver: this will put them out of fear.

QUINCE Well, we will have such a prologue; and it shall be written in eight and six.

BOTTOM No, make it two more; let it be written in eight and eight.

SNOUT Will not the ladies be afeard of the lion?

STARVELING I fear it, I promise you.

BOTTOM Masters, you ought to consider with yourselves: to bring in, God shield us! a lion among ladies is a most dreadful thing: for there is not a more fearful wild-fowl than your lion living; and we ought to look to it.

SNOUT Therefore another prologue must tell he is not a lion.

BOTTOM Nay, you must name his name, and half his face must be seen through the lion's neck; and he himself must speak through, saying thus, or to the same defect,--'Ladies,' or, 'Fair ladies, I would wish you, or, I would request you, or, I would entreat you, not to fear, not to tremble: my life for yours. If you think I come hither as a lion, it were pity of my life. No, I am no such thing; I am a man as other men are:'-- and there, indeed, let him name his name, and tell them plainly he is Snug the joiner.

QUINCE Well, it shall be so. But there is two hard things; that is, to bring the moonlight into a chamber: for, you know, Pyramus and Thisbe meet by moonlight.

SNOUT Doth the moon shine that night we play our play?

BOTTOM A calendar, a calendar! look in the almanack; find out moonshine, find out moonshine.

QUINCE Yes, it doth shine that night.

BOTTOM Why, then may you leave a casement of the great chamber-window, where we play, open; and the moon may shine in at the casement.

QUINCE Ay; or else one must come in with a bush of thorns and a lantern, and say he comes to disfigure or to present the person of moonshine. Then there is another thing: we must have a wall in the great chamber; for Pyramus and Thisby, says the story, did talk through the chink of a wall.

SNOUT You can never bring in a wall.--What say you, Bottom?

BOTTOM Some man or other must present wall: and let him have some plaster, or some loam, or some rough-cast about him, to signify wall; and let him hold his fingers thus, and through that cranny shall Pyramus and Thisby whisper.

QUINCE If that may be, then all is well. Come, sit down, every mother's son, and rehearse your parts. Pyramus, you begin: when you have spoken your speech, enter into that brake; and so every one according to his cue.

[Enter PUCK behind.]

PUCK What hempen homespuns have we swaggering here, So near the cradle of the fairy queen? What, a play toward! I'll be an auditor; An actor too perhaps, if I see cause.

QUINCE Speak, Pyramus.--Thisby, stand forth.

PYRAMUS 'Thisby, the flowers of odious savours sweet,'

QUINCE Odours, odours.

PYRAMUS '--odours savours sweet: So hath thy breath, my dearest Thisby dear.-- But hark, a voice! stay thou but here awhile, And by and by I will to thee appear.'

[Exit.]

PUCK A stranger Pyramus than e'er played here!

[Aside.--Exit.]

THISBE Must I speak now?

QUINCE Ay, marry, must you: for you must understand he goes but to see a noise that he heard, and is to come again.

THISBE 'Most radiant Pyramus, most lily white of hue, Of colour like the red rose on triumphant brier, Most brisky juvenal, and eke most lovely Jew, As true as truest horse, that would never tire, I'll meet thee, Pyramus, at Ninny's tomb.'

QUINCE Ninus' tomb, man: why, you must not speak that yet: that you answer to Pyramus. You speak all your part at once, cues, and all.--Pyramus enter: your cue is past; it is 'never tire.'

[Re-enter PUCK, and BOTTOM with an ass's head.]

THISBE O,'--As true as truest horse, that yet would never tire.'

PYRAMUS 'If I were fair, Thisby, I were only thine:--'

QUINCE O monstrous! O strange! we are haunted. Pray, masters! fly, masters! Help!

[Exeunt Clowns.]

PUCK I'll follow you; I'll lead you about a round, Through bog, through bush, through brake, through brier; Sometime a horse I'll be, sometime a hound, A hog, a headless bear, sometime a fire; And neigh, and bark, and grunt, and roar, and burn, Like horse, hound, hog, bear, fire, at every turn.

[Exit.]

BOTTOM Why do they run away? This is a knavery of them to make me afeard.

[Re-enter SNOUT.]

SNOUT O Bottom, thou art changed! What do I see on thee?

BOTTOM What do you see? you see an ass-head of your own, do you?

[Re-enter QUINCE.]

QUINCE Bless thee, Bottom! bless thee! thou art translated.

[Exit.]

BOTTOM I see their knavery: this is to make an ass of me; to fright me, if they could. But I will not stir from this place, do what they can: I will walk up and down here, and I will sing, that they shall hear I am not afraid.

[Sings.]

The ousel cock, so black of hue, With orange-tawny bill, The throstle with his note so true, The wren with little quill.

TITANIA [Waking.] What angel wakes me from my flowery bed?

BOTTOM [Sings.] The finch, the sparrow, and the lark, The plain-song cuckoo gray, Whose note full many a man doth mark, And dares not answer nay;-- for, indeed, who would set his wit to so foolish a bird? Who would give a bird the lie, though he cry 'cuckoo' never so?

TITANIA I pray thee, gentle mortal, sing again; Mine ear is much enamour'd of thy note. So is mine eye enthralled to thy shape; And thy fair virtue's force perforce doth move me, On the first view, to say, to swear, I love thee.

BOTTOM Methinks, mistress, you should have little reason for that: and yet, to say the truth, reason and love keep little company together now-a-days: the more the pity that some honest neighbours will not make them friends. Nay, I can gleek upon occasion.

TITANIA Thou art as wise as thou art beautiful.

BOTTOM Not so, neither: but if I had wit enough to get out of this wood, I have enough to serve mine own turn.

TITANIA Out of this wood do not desire to go; Thou shalt remain here whether thou wilt or no. I am a spirit of no common rate,-- The summer still doth tend upon my state; And I do love thee: therefore, go with me, I'll give thee fairies to attend on thee; And they shall fetch thee jewels from the deep, And sing, while thou on pressed flowers dost sleep: And I will purge thy mortal grossness so That thou shalt like an airy spirit go.-- Peasblossom! Cobweb! Moth! and Mustardseed!

[Enter Four Fairies.]

FIRST FAIRY Ready.

SECOND FAIRY And I.

THIRD FAIRY And I.

FOURTH FAIRY Where shall we go?

TITANIA Be kind and courteous to this gentleman; Hop in his walks and gambol in his eyes; Feed him with apricocks and dewberries, With purple grapes, green figs, and mulberries; The honey bags steal from the humble-bees, And, for night-tapers, crop their waxen thighs, And light them at the fiery glow-worm's eyes, To have my love to bed and to arise; And pluck the wings from painted butterflies, To fan the moonbeams from his sleeping eyes: Nod to him, elves, and do him courtesies.

FIRST FAIRY Hail, mortal!

SECOND FAIRY Hail!

THIRD FAIRY Hail!

FOURTH FAIRY Hail!

BOTTOM I cry your worships mercy, heartily.--I beseech your worship's name.

COBWEB Cobweb.

BOTTOM I shall desire you of more acquaintance, good Master Cobweb. If I cut my finger, I shall make bold with you.--Your name, honest gentleman?

PEASBLOSSOM Peasblossom.

BOTTOM I pray you, commend me to Mistress Squash, your mother, and to Master Peascod, your father. Good Master Peasblossom, I shall desire you of more acquaintance too.-- Your name, I beseech you, sir?

MUSTARDSEED Mustardseed.

BOTTOM Good Master Mustardseed, I know your patience well: That same cowardly giant-like ox-beef hath devoured many a gentleman of your house: I promise you your kindred hath made my eyes water ere now. I desire you of more acquaintance, good Master Mustardseed.

TITANIA Come, wait upon him; lead him to my bower. The moon, methinks, looks with a watery eye; And when she weeps, weeps every little flower; Lamenting some enforcèd chastity. Tie up my love's tongue, bring him silently.

[Exeunt.]

Scene II

Another part of the wood.

[Enter OBERON.]

OBERON I wonder if Titania be awak'd; Then, what it was that next came in her eye, Which she must dote on in extremity.

[Enter PUCK.]

Here comes my messenger.--How now, mad spirit? What night-rule now about this haunted grove?

PUCK My mistress with a monster is in love. Near to her close and consecrated bower, While she was in her dull and sleeping hour, A crew of patches, rude mechanicals, That work for bread upon Athenian stalls, Were met together to rehearse a play Intended for great Theseus' nuptial day. The shallowest thickskin of that barren sort Who Pyramus presented in their sport, Forsook his Scene and enter'd in a brake; When I did him at this advantage take, An ass's nowl I fixèd on his head; Anon, his Thisbe must be answered, And forth my mimic comes. When they him spy, As wild geese that the creeping fowler eye, Or russet-pated choughs, many in sort, Rising and cawing at the gun's report, Sever themselves and madly sweep the sky, So at his sight away his fellows fly: And at our stamp here, o'er and o'er one falls; He murder cries, and help from Athens calls. Their sense thus weak, lost with their fears, thus strong, Made senseless things begin to do them wrong; For briers and thorns at their apparel snatch; Some sleeves, some hats: from yielders all things catch. I led them on in this distracted fear, And left sweet Pyramus translated there: When in that moment,--so it came to pass,-- Titania wak'd, and straightway lov'd an ass.

OBERON This falls out better than I could devise. But hast thou yet latch'd the Athenian's eyes With the love-juice, as I did bid thee do?

PUCK I took him sleeping,--that is finish'd too,-- And the Athenian woman by his side; That, when he wak'd, of force she must be ey'd.

[Enter DEMETRIUS and HERMIA.]

OBERON Stand close; this is the same Athenian.

PUCK This is the woman, but not this the man.

DEMETRIUS O, why rebuke you him that loves you so? Lay breath so bitter on your bitter foe.

HERMIA Now I but chide, but I should use thee worse; For thou, I fear, hast given me cause to curse. If thou hast slain Lysander in his sleep, Being o'er shoes in blood, plunge in the deep, And kill me too. The sun was not so true unto the day As he to me: would he have stol'n away From sleeping Hermia? I'll believe as soon This whole earth may be bor'd; and that the moon May through the centre creep and so displease Her brother's noontide with the antipodes. It cannot be but thou hast murder'd him; So should a murderer look; so dead, so grim.

DEMETRIUS So should the murder'd look; and so should I, Pierc'd through the heart with your stern cruelty: Yet you, the murderer, look as bright, as clear, As yonder Venus in her glimmering sphere.

HERMIA What's this to my Lysander? where is he? Ah, good Demetrius, wilt thou give him me?

DEMETRIUS I had rather give his carcass to my hounds.

HERMIA Out, dog! out, cur! thou driv'st me past the bounds
Of maiden's patience. Hast thou slain him, then? Henceforth
be never number'd among men! Oh! once tell true; tell true,
even for my sake; Durst thou have look'd upon him, being
awake, And hast thou kill'd him sleeping? O brave touch!
Could not a worm, an adder, do so much? An adder did it; for
with doubler tongue Than thine, thou serpent, never adder
stung.

DEMETRIUS You spend your passion on a mispris'd mood: I
am not guilty of Lysander's blood; Nor is he dead, for aught
that I can tell.

HERMIA I pray thee, tell me, then, that he is well.

DEMETRIUS An if I could, what should I get therefore?

HERMIA A privilege never to see me more.-- And from thy
hated presence part I so: See me no more whether he be dead
or no.

[Exit.]

DEMETRIUS There is no following her in this fierce vein:
Here, therefore, for a while I will remain. So sorrow's
heaviness doth heavier grow For debt that bankrupt sleep
doth sorrow owe; Which now in some slight measure it will
pay, If for his tender here I make some stay.

[Lies down.]

OBERON What hast thou done? thou hast mistaken quite, And laid the love-juice on some true-love's sight: Of thy misprision must perforce ensue Some true love turn'd, and not a false turn'd true.

PUCK Then fate o'er-rules, that, one man holding troth, A million fail, confounding oath on oath.

OBERON About the wood go, swifter than the wind, And Helena of Athens look thou find: All fancy-sick she is, and pale of cheer, With sighs of love, that costs the fresh blood dear. By some illusion see thou bring her here; I'll charm his eyes against she do appear.

PUCK I go, I go; look how I go,-- Swifter than arrow from the Tartar's bow.

[Exit.]

OBERON Flower of this purple dye, Hit with Cupid's archery, Sink in apple of his eye! When his love he doth espy, Let her shine as gloriously As the Venus of the sky.-- When thou wak'st, if she be by, Beg of her for remedy.

[Re-enter PUCK.]

PUCK Captain of our fairy band, Helena is here at hand, And the youth mistook by me Pleading for a lover's fee; Shall we their fond pageant see? Lord, what fools these mortals be!

OBERON Stand aside: the noise they make Will cause Demetrius to awake.

PUCK Then will two at once woo one,-- That must needs be sport alone; And those things do best please me That befall preposterously.

[Enter LYSANDER and HELENA.]

LYSANDER Why should you think that I should woo in scorn? Scorn and derision never come in tears. Look when I vow, I weep; and vows so born, In their nativity all truth appears. How can these things in me seem scorn to you, Bearing the badge of faith, to prove them true?

HELENA You do advance your cunning more and more. When truth kills truth, O devilish-holy fray! These vows are Hermia's: will you give her o'er? Weigh oath with oath, and you will nothing weigh: Your vows to her and me, put in two scales, Will even weigh; and both as light as tales.

LYSANDER I had no judgment when to her I swore.

HELENA Nor none, in my mind, now you give her o'er.

LYSANDER Demetrius loves her, and he loves not you.

DEMETRIUS [Awaking.] O Helen, goddess, nymph, perfect, divine! To what, my love, shall I compare thine eyne? Crystal is muddy. O, how ripe in show Thy lips, those kissing cherries, tempting grow! That pure congealed white, high Taurus' snow, Fann'd with the eastern wind, turns to a crow When thou hold'st up thy hand: O, let me kiss This princess of pure white, this seal of bliss!

HELENA O spite! O hell! I see you all are bent To set against me for your merriment. If you were civil, and knew courtesy, You would not do me thus much injury. Can you not hate me, as I know you do, But you must join in souls to mock me too? If you were men, as men you are in show, You would not use a gentle lady so; To vow, and swear, and superpraise my parts, When I am sure you hate me with your hearts. You both are rivals, and love Hermia; And now both rivals, to mock Helena: A trim exploit, a manly enterprise, To conjure tears up in a poor maid's eyes With your derision! None of noble sort Would so offend a virgin, and extort A poor soul's patience, all to make you sport.

LYSANDER You are unkind, Demetrius; be not so; For you love Hermia: this you know I know: And here, with all good will, with all my heart, In Hermia's love I yield you up my part; And yours of Helena to me bequeath, Whom I do love and will do till my death.

HELENA Never did mockers waste more idle breath.

DEMETRIUS Lysander, keep thy Hermia; I will none: If e'er I lov'd her, all that love is gone. My heart to her but as guest-wise sojourn'd; And now to Helen is it home return'd, There to remain.

LYSANDER Helen, it is not so.

DEMETRIUS Disparage not the faith thou dost not know, Lest, to thy peril, thou aby it dear.-- Look where thy love comes; yonder is thy dear.

[Enter HERMIA.]

HERMIA Dark night, that from the eye his function takes, The ear more quick of apprehension makes; Wherein it doth impair the seeing sense, It pays the hearing double recompense:-- Thou art not by mine eye, Lysander, found; Mine ear, I thank it, brought me to thy sound. But why unkindly didst thou leave me so?

LYSANDER Why should he stay whom love doth press to go?

HERMIA What love could press Lysander from my side?

LYSANDER Lysander's love, that would not let him bide,-- Fair Helena,--who more engilds the night Than all yon fiery oes and eyes of light. Why seek'st thou me? could not this make thee know The hate I bare thee made me leave thee so?

HERMIA You speak not as you think; it cannot be.

HELENA Lo, she is one of this confederacy! Now I perceive they have conjoin'd all three To fashion this false sport in spite of me. Injurious Hermia! most ungrateful maid! Have you conspir'd, have you with these contriv'd, To bait me with this foul derision? Is all the counsel that we two have shar'd, The sisters' vows, the hours that we have spent, When we have chid the hasty-footed time For parting us,--O, is all forgot? All school-days' friendship, childhood innocence? We, Hermia, like two artificial gods, Have with our needles created both one flower, Both on one sampler, sitting on one cushion, Both warbling of one song, both in one key; As if our hands, our sides, voices, and minds, Had been incorporate. So we grew together, Like to a double cherry, seeming parted; But yet a union in partition, Two lovely berries moulded on one stem: So, with two seeming bodies, but one heart; Two of the first, like coats in heraldry, Due but to one, and crowned with one crest. And will you rent our ancient love asunder, To join with men in scorning your poor friend? It is not friendly, 'tis not maidenly: Our sex, as well as I, may chide you for it, Though I alone do feel the injury.

HERMIA I am amazed at your passionate words: I scorn you not; it seems that you scorn me.

HELENA Have you not set Lysander, as in scorn, To follow me, and praise my eyes and face? And made your other love, Demetrius,-- Who even but now did spurn me with his foot,-- To call me goddess, nymph, divine, and rare, Precious, celestial? Wherefore speaks he this To her he hates? and wherefore doth Lysander Deny your love, so rich within his soul, And tender me, forsooth, affection, But by your setting on, by your consent? What though I be not so in grace as you, So hung upon with love, so fortunate; But miserable most, to love unlov'd? This you should pity rather than despise.

HERMIA I understand not what you mean by this.

HELENA Ay, do persever, counterfeit sad looks, Make mows upon me when I turn my back; Wink each at other; hold the sweet jest up: This sport, well carried, shall be chronicled. If you have any pity, grace, or manners, You would not make me such an argument. But fare ye well: 'tis partly my own fault; Which death, or absence, soon shall remedy.

LYSANDER Stay, gentle Helena; hear my excuse; My love, my life, my soul, fair Helena!

HELENA O excellent!

HERMIA Sweet, do not scorn her so.

DEMETRIUS If she cannot entreat, I can compel.

LYSANDER Thou canst compel no more than she entreat; Thy threats have no more strength than her weak prayers.-- Helen, I love thee; by my life I do; I swear by that which I will lose for thee To prove him false that says I love thee not.

DEMETRIUS I say I love thee more than he can do.

LYSANDER If thou say so, withdraw, and prove it too.

DEMETRIUS Quick, come,--

HERMIA Lysander, whereto tends all this?

LYSANDER Away, you Ethiope!

DEMETRIUS No, no, sir:--he will Seem to break loose; take on as you would follow: But yet come not. You are a tame man; go!

LYSANDER Hang off, thou cat, thou burr: vile thing, let loose, Or I will shake thee from me like a serpent.

HERMIA Why are you grown so rude? what change is this, Sweet love?

LYSANDER Thy love! out, tawny Tartar, out! Out, loathed medicine! hated potion, hence!

HERMIA Do you not jest?

HELENA Yes, sooth; and so do you.

LYSANDER Demetrius, I will keep my word with thee.

DEMETRIUS I would I had your bond; for I perceive A weak bond holds you; I'll not trust your word.

LYSANDER What! should I hurt her, strike her, kill her dead? Although I hate her, I'll not harm her so.

HERMIA What! can you do me greater harm than hate? Hate me! wherefore? O me! what news, my love? Am not I Hermia? Are not you Lysander? I am as fair now as I was erewhile. Since night you lov'd me; yet since night you left me: Why then, you left me,--O, the gods forbid!-- In earnest, shall I say?

LYSANDER Ay, by my life; And never did desire to see thee more. Therefore be out of hope, of question, doubt, Be certain, nothing truer; 'tis no jest That I do hate thee and love Helena.

HERMIA O me! you juggler! you cankerblossom! You thief of love! What! have you come by night, And stol'n my love's heart from him?

HELENA Fine, i' faith! Have you no modesty, no maiden shame, No touch of bashfulness? What! will you tear Impatient answers from my gentle tongue? Fie, fie! you counterfeit, you puppet, you!

HERMIA Puppet! why so? Ay, that way goes the game. Now I perceive that she hath made compare Between our statures; she hath urg'd her height; And with her personage, her tall personage, Her height, forsooth, she hath prevail'd with him.-- And are you grown so high in his esteem Because I am so dwarfish and so low? How low am I, thou painted maypole? speak; How low am I? I am not yet so low But that my nails can reach unto thine eyes.

HELENA I pray you, though you mock me, gentlemen, Let her not hurt me. I was never curst; I have no gift at all in shrewishness; I am a right maid for my cowardice; Let her not strike me. You perhaps may think, Because she is something lower than myself, That I can match her.

HERMIA Lower! hark, again.

HELENA Good Hermia, do not be so bitter with me. I evermore did love you, Hermia; Did ever keep your counsels; never wrong'd you; Save that, in love unto Demetrius, I told him of your stealth unto this wood: He follow'd you; for love I follow'd him; But he hath chid me hence, and threaten'd me To strike me, spurn me, nay, to kill me too: And now, so you will let me quiet go, To Athens will I bear my folly back, And follow you no farther. Let me go: You see how simple and how fond I am.

HERMIA Why, get you gone: who is't that hinders you?

HELENA A foolish heart that I leave here behind.

HERMIA What! with Lysander?

HELENA With Demetrius.

LYSANDER Be not afraid; she shall not harm thee, Helena.

DEMETRIUS No, sir, she shall not, though you take her part.

HELENA O, when she's angry, she is keen and shrewd: She was a vixen when she went to school; And, though she be but little, she is fierce.

HERMIA Little again! nothing but low and little!-- Why will you suffer her to flout me thus? Let me come to her.

LYSANDER Get you gone, you dwarf; You minimus, of hind'ring knot-grass made; You bead, you acorn.

DEMETRIUS You are too officious In her behalf that scorns your services. Let her alone: speak not of Helena; Take not her part; for if thou dost intend Never so little show of love to her, Thou shalt aby it.

LYSANDER Now she holds me not; Now follow, if thou dar'st, to try whose right, Of thine or mine, is most in Helena.

DEMETRIUS Follow! nay, I'll go with thee, cheek by jole.

[Exeunt LYSANDER and DEMETRIUS.]

HERMIA You, mistress, all this coil is 'long of you: Nay, go not back.

HELENA I will not trust you, I; Nor longer stay in your curst company. Your hands than mine are quicker for a fray; My legs are longer though, to run away.

[Exit.]

HERMIA I am amaz'd, and know not what to say.

[Exit, pursuing HELENA.]

OBERON This is thy negligence: still thou mistak'st, Or else commit'st thy knaveries willfully.

PUCK Believe me, king of shadows, I mistook. Did not you tell me I should know the man By the Athenian garments he had on? And so far blameless proves my enterprise That I have 'nointed an Athenian's eyes: And so far am I glad it so did sort, As this their jangling I esteem a sport.

OBERON Thou seest these lovers seek a place to fight; Hie therefore, Robin, overcast the night; The starry welkin cover thou anon With drooping fog, as black as Acheron, And lead these testy rivals so astray As one come not within another's way. Like to Lysander sometime frame thy tongue, Then stir Demetrius up with bitter wrong; And sometime rail thou like Demetrius; And from each other look thou lead them thus, Till o'er their brows death-counterfeiting sleep With leaden legs and batty wings doth creep: Then crush this herb into Lysander's eye; Whose liquor hath this virtuous property, To take from thence all error with his might And make his eyeballs roll with wonted sight. When they next wake, all this derision Shall seem a dream and fruitless vision; And back to Athens shall the lovers wend With league whose date till death shall never end. Whiles I in this affair do thee employ, I'll to my queen, and beg her Indian boy; And then I will her charmed eye release From monster's view, and all things shall be peace.

PUCK My fairy lord, this must be done with haste, For night's swift dragons cut the clouds full fast; And yonder shines Aurora's harbinger, At whose approach ghosts, wandering here and there, Troop home to churchyards: damned spirits all, That in cross-ways and floods have burial, Already to their wormy beds are gone; For fear lest day should look their shames upon They wilfully exile themselves from light, And must for aye consort with black-brow'd night.

OBERON But we are spirits of another sort: I with the morning's love have oft made sport; And, like a forester, the groves may tread Even till the eastern gate, all fiery-red, Opening on Neptune with fair blessed beams, Turns into yellow gold his salt-green streams. But, notwithstanding, haste; make no delay: We may effect this business yet ere day.

[Exit OBERON.]

PUCK Up and down, up and down; I will lead them up and down: I am fear'd in field and town. Goblin, lead them up and down. Here comes one.

[Enter LYSANDER.]

LYSANDER Where art thou, proud Demetrius? speak thou now.

PUCK Here, villain; drawn and ready. Where art thou?

LYSANDER I will be with thee straight.

PUCK Follow me, then, To plainer ground.

[Exit LYSANDER as following the voice.]

[Enter DEMETRIUS.]

DEMETRIUS Lysander! speak again. Thou runaway, thou coward, art thou fled? Speak. In some bush? where dost thou hide thy head?

PUCK Thou coward, art thou bragging to the stars, Telling the bushes that thou look'st for wars, And wilt not come? Come, recreant; come, thou child; I'll whip thee with a rod: he is defiled That draws a sword on thee.

DEMETRIUS Yea, art thou there?

PUCK Follow my voice; we'll try no manhood here.

[Exeunt.]

[Re-enter LYSANDER.]

LYSANDER He goes before me, and still dares me on; When I come where he calls, then he is gone. The villain is much lighter heeled than I: I follow'd fast, but faster he did fly; That fallen am I in dark uneven way, And here will rest me. Come, thou gentle day! [Lies down.] For if but once thou show me thy grey light, I'll find Demetrius, and revenge this spite.

[Sleeps.]

[Re-enter PUCK and DEMETRIUS.]

PUCK Ho, ho, ho, ho! Coward, why com'st thou not?

DEMETRIUS Abide me, if thou dar'st; for well I wot Thou runn'st before me, shifting every place; And dar'st not stand, nor look me in the face. Where art thou?

PUCK Come hither; I am here.

DEMETRIUS Nay, then, thou mock'st me. Thou shalt buy this dear, If ever I thy face by daylight see: Now, go thy way. Faintness constraineth me To measure out my length on this cold bed.-- By day's approach look to be visited.

[Lies down and sleeps.]

[Enter HELENA.]

HELENA O weary night, O long and tedious night, Abate thy hours! Shine comforts from the east, That I may back to Athens by daylight, From these that my poor company detest:-- And sleep, that sometimes shuts up sorrow's eye, Steal me awhile from mine own company.

[Sleeps.]

PUCK Yet but three? Come one more; Two of both kinds makes up four. Here she comes, curst and sad:-- Cupid is a knavish lad, Thus to make poor females mad.

[Enter HERMIA.]

HERMIA Never so weary, never so in woe, Bedabbled with the dew, and torn with briers; I can no further crawl, no further go; My legs can keep no pace with my desires. Here will I rest me till the break of day. Heavens shield Lysander, if they mean a fray!

[Lies down.]

PUCK On the ground Sleep sound: I'll apply To your eye, Gentle lover, remedy.

[Squeezing the juice on LYSANDER'S eye.]

When thou wak'st, Thou tak'st True delight In the sight Of thy former lady's eye: And the country proverb known, That every man should take his own, In your waking shall be shown: Jack shall have Jill; Nought shall go ill; The man shall have his mare again, and all shall be well.

[Exit PUCK.--DEMETRIUS, HELENA &c, sleep.]

Act IV

Scene I

The Wood.

[Enter TITANIA and BOTTOM; PEASBLOSSOM, COBWEB, MOTH, MUSTARDSEED, and other FAIRIES attending; OBERON behind, unseen.]

TITANIA Come, sit thee down upon this flowery bed, While I thy amiable cheeks do coy, And stick musk-roses in thy sleek smooth head, And kiss thy fair large ears, my gentle joy.

BOTTOM Where's Peasblossom?

PEASBLOSSOM Ready.

BOTTOM Scratch my head, Peasblossom.-- Where's Monsieur Cobweb?

COBWEB Ready.

BOTTOM Monsieur Cobweb; good monsieur, get you your weapons in your hand and kill me a red-hipped humble-bee on the top of a thistle; and, good monsieur, bring me the honey-bag. Do not fret yourself too much in the action, monsieur; and, good monsieur, have a care the honey-bag break not; I would be loath to have you overflown with a honey-bag, signior.-- Where's Monsieur Mustardseed?

MUSTARDSEED Ready.

BOTTOM Give me your neif, Monsieur Mustardseed. Pray you, leave your curtsy, good monsieur.

MUSTARDSEED What's your will?

BOTTOM Nothing, good monsieur, but to help Cavalero Cobweb to scratch. I must to the barber's, monsieur; for methinks I am marvellous hairy about the face; and I am such a tender ass, if my hair do but tickle me I must scratch.

TITANIA What, wilt thou hear some music, my sweet love?

BOTTOM I have a reasonable good ear in music; let us have the tongs and the bones.

TITANIA Or say, sweet love, what thou desirest to eat.

BOTTOM Truly, a peck of provender; I could munch your good dry oats. Methinks I have a great desire to a bottle of hay: good hay, sweet hay, hath no fellow.

TITANIA I have a venturous fairy that shall seek The squirrel's hoard, and fetch thee new nuts.

BOTTOM I had rather have a handful or two of dried peas. But, I pray you, let none of your people stir me; I have an exposition of sleep come upon me.

TITANIA Sleep thou, and I will wind thee in my arms. Fairies, be gone, and be all ways away. So doth the woodbine the sweet honeysuckle Gently entwist,--the female ivy so Enrings the barky fingers of the elm. O, how I love thee! how I dote on thee!

[They sleep.]

[OBERON advances. Enter PUCK.]

OBERON Welcome, good Robin. Seest thou this sweet sight? Her dotage now I do begin to pity. For, meeting her of late behind the wood, Seeking sweet favours for this hateful fool, I did upbraid her and fall out with her: For she his hairy temples then had rounded With coronet of fresh and fragrant flowers; And that same dew, which sometime on the buds Was wont to swell like round and orient pearls, Stood now within the pretty flow'rets' eyes, Like tears that did their own disgrace bewail. When I had, at my pleasure, taunted her, And she, in mild terms, begg'd my patience, I then did ask of her her changeling child; Which straight she gave me, and her fairy sent To bear him to my bower in fairy-land. And now I have the boy, I will undo This hateful imperfection of her eyes. And, gentle Puck, take this transformed scalp From off the head of this Athenian swain, That he awaking when the other do, May all to Athens back again repair, And think no more of this night's accidents But as the fierce vexation of a dream. But first I will release the fairy queen. Be as thou wast wont to be; [Touching her eyes with an herb.] See as thou was wont to see. Dian's bud o'er Cupid's flower Hath such force and blessed power. Now, my Titania; wake you, my sweet queen.

TITANIA My Oberon! what visions have I seen! Methought I was enamour'd of an ass.

OBERON There lies your love.

TITANIA How came these things to pass? O, how mine eyes do loathe his visage now!

OBERON Silence awhile.--Robin, take off this head. Titania, music call; and strike more dead Than common sleep, of all these five, the sense.

TITANIA Music, ho! music; such as charmeth sleep.

PUCK Now when thou wak'st, with thine own fool's eyes peep.

OBERON Sound, music. [Still music.] Come, my queen, take hands with me, And rock the ground whereon these sleepers be. Now thou and I are new in amity, And will to-morrow midnight solemnly Dance in Duke Theseus' house triumphantly, And bless it to all fair prosperity: There shall the pairs of faithful lovers be Wedded, with Theseus, all in jollity.

PUCK Fairy king, attend and mark; I do hear the morning lark.

OBERON Then, my queen, in silence sad, Trip we after night's shade. We the globe can compass soon, Swifter than the wand'ring moon.

TITANIA Come, my lord; and in our flight, Tell me how it came this night That I sleeping here was found With these mortals on the ground.

[Exeunt. Horns sound within.]

[Enter THESEUS, HIPPOLYTA, EGEUS, and Train.]

THESEUS Go, one of you, find out the forester;-- For now our observation is perform'd; And since we have the vaward of the day, My love shall hear the music of my hounds,-- Uncouple in the western valley; go:-- Despatch, I say, and find the forester.--

[Exit an ATTENDANT.]

We will, fair queen, up to the mountain's top, And mark the musical confusion Of hounds and echo in conjunction.

HIPPOLYTA I was with Hercules and Cadmus once When in a wood of Crete they bay'd the bear With hounds of Sparta: never did I hear Such gallant chiding; for, besides the groves, The skies, the fountains, every region near Seem'd all one mutual cry: I never heard So musical a discord, such sweet thunder.

THESEUS My hounds are bred out of the Spartan kind, So flew'd, so sanded; and their heads are hung With ears that sweep away the morning dew; Crook-knee'd and dew-lap'd like Thessalian bulls; Slow in pursuit, but match'd in mouth like bells, Each under each. A cry more tuneable Was never holla'd to, nor cheer'd with horn, In Crete, in Sparta, nor in Thessaly. Judge when you hear.--But, soft, what nymphs are these?

EGEUS My lord, this is my daughter here asleep; And this Lysander; this Demetrius is; This Helena, old Nedar's Helena: I wonder of their being here together.

THESEUS No doubt they rose up early to observe The rite of May; and, hearing our intent, Came here in grace of our solemnity.-- But speak, Egeus; is not this the day That Hermia should give answer of her choice?

EGEUS It is, my lord.

THESEUS Go, bid the huntsmen wake them with their horns.

[Horns, and shout within. DEMETRIUS, LYSANDER,HERMIA, and HELENA awake and start up.]

Good-morrow, friends. Saint Valentine is past; Begin these wood-birds but to couple now?

LYSANDER Pardon, my lord.

[He and the rest kneel to THESEUS.]

THESEUS I pray you all, stand up. I know you two are rival enemies; How comes this gentle concord in the world, That hatred is so far from jealousy To sleep by hate, and fear no enmity?

LYSANDER My lord, I shall reply amazedly, Half 'sleep, half waking; but as yet, I swear, I cannot truly say how I came here: But, as I think,--for truly would I speak-- And now I do bethink me, so it is,-- I came with Hermia hither: our intent Was to be gone from Athens, where we might be, Without the peril of the Athenian law.

EGEUS Enough, enough, my lord; you have enough; I beg the law, the law upon his head.-- They would have stol'n away, they would, Demetrius, Thereby to have defeated you and me: You of your wife, and me of my consent,-- Of my consent that she should be your wife.

DEMETRIUS My lord, fair Helen told me of their stealth, Of this their purpose hither to this wood; And I in fury hither follow'd them, Fair Helena in fancy following me. But, my good lord, I wot not by what power,-- But by some power it is,--my love to Hermia, Melted as the snow--seems to me now As the remembrance of an idle gawd Which in my childhood I did dote upon: And all the faith, the virtue of my heart, The object and the pleasure of mine eye, Is only Helena. To her, my lord, Was I betroth'd ere I saw Hermia: But, like a sickness, did I loathe this food; But, as in health, come to my natural taste, Now I do wish it, love it, long for it, And will for evermore be true to it.

THESEUS Fair lovers, you are fortunately met: Of this discourse we more will hear anon.-- Egeus, I will overbear your will; For in the temple, by and by with us, These couples shall eternally be knit. And, for the morning now is something worn, Our purpos'd hunting shall be set aside.-- Away with us to Athens, three and three, We'll hold a feast in great solemnity.-- Come, Hippolyta.

[Exeunt THESEUS, HIPPOLYTA, EGEUS, and Train.]

DEMETRIUS These things seem small and undistinguishable, Like far-off mountains turned into clouds.

HERMIA Methinks I see these things with parted eye, When every thing seems double.

HELENA So methinks: And I have found Demetrius like a jewel. Mine own, and not mine own.

DEMETRIUS It seems to me That yet we sleep, we dream.--Do not you think The duke was here, and bid us follow him?

HERMIA Yea, and my father.

HELENA And Hippolyta.

LYSANDER And he did bid us follow to the temple.

DEMETRIUS Why, then, we are awake: let's follow him; And by the way let us recount our dreams.

[Exeunt.]

[As they go out, BOTTOM awakes.]

BOTTOM When my cue comes, call me, and I will answer. My next is 'Most fair Pyramus.'--Heigh-ho!--Peter Quince! Flute, the bellows-mender! Snout, the tinker! Starveling! God's my life, stol'n hence, and left me asleep! I have had a most rare vision. I have had a dream--past the wit of man to say what dream it was.--Man is but an ass if he go about to expound this dream. Methought I was--there is no man can tell what. Methought I was, and methought I had,--but man is but a patched fool, if he will offer to say what methought I had. The eye of man hath not heard, the ear of man hath not seen; man's hand is not able to taste, his tongue to conceive, nor his heart to report, what my dream was. I will get Peter Quince to write a ballad of this dream: it shall be called Bottom's Dream, because it hath no bottom; and I will sing it in the latter end of a play, before the duke: peradventure, to make it the more gracious, I shall sing it at her death.

[Exit.]

Scene II

Athens. A Room in QUINCE'S House.

[Enter QUINCE, FLUTE, SNOUT, and STARVELING.]

QUINCE Have you sent to Bottom's house? is he come home yet?

STARVELING He cannot be heard of. Out of doubt, he is transported.

FLUTE If he come not, then the play is marred; it goes not forward, doth it?

QUINCE It is not possible: you have not a man in all Athens able to discharge Pyramus but he.

FLUTE No; he hath simply the best wit of any handicraft man in Athens.

QUINCE Yea, and the best person too: and he is a very paramour for a sweet voice.

FLUTE You must say paragon: a paramour is, God bless us, a thing of naught.

[Enter SNUG.]

SNUG Masters, the duke is coming from the temple; and there is two or three lords and ladies more married: if our sport had gone forward, we had all been made men.

FLUTE O sweet bully Bottom! Thus hath he lost sixpence a day during his life; he could not have 'scaped sixpence a-day; an the duke had not given him sixpence a-day for playing Pyramus, I'll be hanged; he would have deserved it: sixpence a-day in Pyramus, or nothing.

[Enter BOTTOM.]

BOTTOM Where are these lads? where are these hearts?

QUINCE Bottom!--O most courageous day! O most happy hour!

BOTTOM Masters, I am to discourse wonders: but ask me not what; for if I tell you, I am not true Athenian. I will tell you everything, right as it fell out.

QUINCE Let us hear, sweet Bottom.

BOTTOM Not a word of me. All that I will tell you is, that the duke hath dined. Get your apparel together; good strings to your beards, new ribbons to your pumps; meet presently at the palace; every man look over his part; for the short and the long is, our play is preferred. In any case, let Thisby have clean linen; and let not him that plays the lion pare his nails, for they shall hang out for the lion's claws. And, most dear actors, eat no onions nor garlick, for we are to utter sweet breath; and I do not doubt but to hear them say it is a sweet comedy. No more words: away! go; away!

[Exeunt.]

Act V

Scene I

Athens. An Apartment in the Palace of THESEUS.

[Enter THESEUS, HIPPOLYTA, PHILOSTRATE, Lords, and Attendants.]

HIPPOLYTA 'Tis strange, my Theseus, that these lovers speak of.

THESEUS More strange than true. I never may believe These antique fables, nor these fairy toys. Lovers and madmen have such seething brains, Such shaping fantasies, that apprehend More than cool reason ever comprehends. The lunatic, the lover, and the poet Are of imagination all compact: One sees more devils than vast hell can hold; That is the madman: the lover, all as frantic, Sees Helen's beauty in a brow of Egypt: The poet's eye, in a fine frenzy rolling, Doth glance from heaven to earth, from earth to heaven; And as imagination bodies forth The forms of things unknown, the poet's pen Turns them to shapes, and gives to airy nothing A local habitation and a name. Such tricks hath strong imagination, That, if it would but apprehend some joy, It comprehends some bringer of that joy; Or in the night, imagining some fear, How easy is a bush supposed a bear?

HIPPOLYTA But all the story of the night told over, And all their minds transfigur'd so together, More witnesseth than fancy's images, And grows to something of great constancy; But, howsoever, strange and admirable.

202

[Enter LYSANDER, DEMETRIUS, HERMIA, and HELENA.]

THESEUS Here come the lovers, full of joy and mirth.-- Joy, gentle friends! joy and fresh days of love Accompany your hearts!

LYSANDER More than to us Wait in your royal walks, your board, your bed!

THESEUS Come now; what masques, what dances shall we have, To wear away this long age of three hours Between our after-supper and bed-time? Where is our usual manager of mirth? What revels are in hand? Is there no play To ease the anguish of a torturing hour? Call Philostrate.

PHILOSTRATE Here, mighty Theseus.

THESEUS Say, what abridgment have you for this evening? What masque? what music? How shall we beguile The lazy time, if not with some delight?

PHILOSTRATE There is a brief how many sports are ripe; Make choice of which your highness will see first.

[Giving a paper.]

THESEUS [Reads.] 'The battle with the Centaurs, to be sung By an Athenian eunuch to the harp.' We'll none of that: that have I told my love, In glory of my kinsman Hercules. 'The riot of the tipsy Bacchanals, Tearing the Thracian singer in their rage.' That is an old device, and it was play'd When I from Thebes came last a conqueror. 'The thrice three Muses mourning for the death Of learning, late deceas'd in beggary.' That is some satire, keen and critical, Not sorting with a nuptial ceremony. 'A tedious brief Scene of young Pyramus And his love Thisbe; very tragical mirth.' Merry and tragical! tedious and brief! That is hot ice and wondrous strange snow. How shall we find the concord of this discord?

PHILOSTRATE A play there is, my lord, some ten words long, Which is as brief as I have known a play; But by ten words, my lord, it is too long, Which makes it tedious: for in all the play There is not one word apt, one player fitted: And tragical, my noble lord, it is; For Pyramus therein doth kill himself: Which when I saw rehears'd, I must confess, Made mine eyes water; but more merry tears The passion of loud laughter never shed.

THESEUS What are they that do play it?

PHILOSTRATE Hard-handed men that work in Athens here, Which never labour'd in their minds till now; And now have toil'd their unbreath'd memories With this same play against your nuptial.

THESEUS And we will hear it.

PHILOSTRATE No, my noble lord, It is not for you: I have heard it over, And it is nothing, nothing in the world; Unless you can find sport in their intents, Extremely stretch'd and conn'd with cruel pain, To do you service.

THESEUS I will hear that play; For never anything can be amiss When simpleness and duty tender it. Go, bring them in: and take your places, ladies.

[Exit PHILOSTRATE.]

HIPPOLYTA I love not to see wretchedness o'er-charged, And duty in his service perishing.

THESEUS Why, gentle sweet, you shall see no such thing.

HIPPOLYTA He says they can do nothing in this kind.

THESEUS The kinder we, to give them thanks for nothing. Our sport shall be to take what they mistake: And what poor duty cannot do, Noble respect takes it in might, not merit. Where I have come, great clerks have purposed To greet me with premeditated welcomes; Where I have seen them shiver and look pale, Make periods in the midst of sentences, Throttle their practis'd accent in their fears, And, in conclusion, dumbly have broke off, Not paying me a welcome. Trust me, sweet, Out of this silence yet I pick'd a welcome; And in the modesty of fearful duty I read as much as from the rattling tongue Of saucy and audacious eloquence. Love, therefore, and tongue-tied simplicity In least speak most to my capacity.

[Enter PHILOSTRATE.]

PHILOSTRATE So please your grace, the prologue is address'd.

THESEUS Let him approach.

[Flourish of trumpets. Enter PROLOGUE.]

PROLOGUE 'If we offend, it is with our good will. That you should think, we come not to offend, But with good will. To show our simple skill, That is the true beginning of our end. Consider then, we come but in despite. We do not come, as minding to content you, Our true intent is. All for your delight We are not here. That you should here repent you, The actors are at hand: and, by their show, You shall know all that you are like to know,'

THESEUS This fellow doth not stand upon points.

LYSANDER He hath rid his prologue like a rough colt; he knows not the stop. A good moral, my lord: it is not enough to speak, but to speak true.

HIPPOLYTA Indeed he hath played on this prologue like a child on a recorder; a sound, but not in government.

THESEUS His speech was like a tangled chain; nothing impaired, but all disordered. Who is next?

[Enter PYRAMUS and THISBE, WALL, MOONSHINE, and LION, as in dumb show.]

PROLOGUE Gentles, perchance you wonder at this show; But wonder on, till truth make all things plain. This man is Pyramus, if you would know; This beauteous lady Thisby is certain. This man, with lime and rough-cast, doth present Wall, that vile Wall which did these lovers sunder; And through Wall's chink, poor souls, they are content To whisper, at the which let no man wonder. This man, with lanthorn, dog, and bush of thorn, Presenteth Moonshine: for, if you will know, By moonshine did these lovers think no scorn To meet at Ninus' tomb, there, there to woo. This grisly beast, which by name Lion hight, The trusty Thisby, coming first by night, Did scare away, or rather did affright; And as she fled, her mantle she did fall; Which Lion vile with bloody mouth did stain: Anon comes Pyramus, sweet youth, and tall, And finds his trusty Thisby's mantle slain; Whereat with blade, with bloody blameful blade, He bravely broach'd his boiling bloody breast; And Thisby, tarrying in mulberry shade, His dagger drew, and died. For all the rest, Let Lion, Moonshine, Wall, and lovers twain, At large discourse while here they do remain.

[Exeunt PROLOGUE, THISBE, LION, and MOONSHINE.]

THESEUS I wonder if the lion be to speak.

DEMETRIUS No wonder, my lord: one lion may, when many asses do.

WALL In this same interlude it doth befall That I, one Snout by name, present a wall: And such a wall as I would have you think That had in it a crannied hole or chink, Through which the lovers, Pyramus and Thisby, Did whisper often very secretly. This loam, this rough-cast, and this stone, doth show That I am that same wall; the truth is so: And this the cranny is, right and sinister, Through which the fearful lovers are to whisper.

THESEUS Would you desire lime and hair to speak better?

DEMETRIUS It is the wittiest partition that ever I heard discourse, my lord.

THESEUS Pyramus draws near the wall; silence.

[Enter PYRAMUS.]

PYRAMUS O grim-look'd night! O night with hue so black! O night, which ever art when day is not! O night, O night, alack, alack, alack, I fear my Thisby's promise is forgot!-- And thou, O wall, O sweet, O lovely wall, That stand'st between her father's ground and mine; Thou wall, O wall, O sweet and lovely wall, Show me thy chink, to blink through with mine eyne.

[WALL holds up his fingers.]

Thanks, courteous wall: Jove shield thee well for this! But what see what see I? No Thisby do I see. O wicked wall, through whom I see no bliss, Curs'd be thy stones for thus deceiving me!

THESEUS The wall, methinks, being sensible, should curse again.

PYRAMUS No, in truth, sir, he should not. 'Deceiving me' is Thisby's cue: she is to enter now, and I am to spy her through the wall. You shall see it will fall pat as I told you.--Yonder she comes.

[Enter THISBE.]

THISBE O wall, full often hast thou heard my moans, For parting my fair Pyramus and me: My cherry lips have often kiss'd thy stones: Thy stones with lime and hair knit up in thee.

PYRAMUS I see a voice; now will I to the chink, To spy an I can hear my Thisby's face. Thisby!

THISBE My love! thou art my love, I think.

PYRAMUS Think what thou wilt, I am thy lover's grace; And like Limander am I trusty still.

THISBE And I like Helen, till the fates me kill.

PYRAMUS Not Shafalus to Procrus was so true.

THISBE As Shafalus to Procrus, I to you.

PYRAMUS O, kiss me through the hole of this vile wall.

THISBE I kiss the wall's hole, not your lips at all.

PYRAMUS Wilt thou at Ninny's tomb meet me straightway?

THISBE 'Tide life, 'tide death, I come without delay.

WALL Thus have I, wall, my part discharged so; And, being done, thus Wall away doth go.

[Exeunt WALL, PYRAMUS and THISBE.]

THESEUS Now is the mural down between the two neighbours.

DEMETRIUS No remedy, my lord, when walls are so wilful to hear without warning.

HIPPOLYTA This is the silliest stuff that ever I heard.

THESEUS The best in this kind are but shadows; and the worst are no worse, if imagination amend them.

HIPPOLYTA It must be your imagination then, and not theirs.

THESEUS If we imagine no worse of them than they of themselves, they may pass for excellent men. Here come two noble beasts in, a moon and a lion.

[Enter LION and MOONSHINE.]

LION You, ladies, you, whose gentle hearts do fear The smallest monstrous mouse that creeps on floor, May now, perchance, both quake and tremble here, When lion rough in wildest rage doth roar. Then know that I, one Snug the joiner, am A lion fell, nor else no lion's dam: For, if I should as lion come in strife Into this place, 'twere pity on my life.

THESEUS A very gentle beast, and of a good conscience.

DEMETRIUS The very best at a beast, my lord, that e'er I saw.

LYSANDER This lion is a very fox for his valour.

THESEUS True; and a goose for his discretion.

DEMETRIUS Not so, my lord; for his valour cannot carry his discretion, and the fox carries the goose.

THESEUS His discretion, I am sure, cannot carry his valour; for the goose carries not the fox. It is well; leave it to his discretion, and let us listen to the moon.

MOONSHINE This lanthorn doth the horned moon present:

DEMETRIUS He should have worn the horns on his head.

THESEUS He is no crescent, and his horns are invisible within the circumference.

MOONSHINE This lanthorn doth the horned moon present; Myself the man i' the moon do seem to be.

THESEUS This is the greatest error of all the rest: the man should be put into the lantern. How is it else the man i' the moon?

DEMETRIUS He dares not come there for the candle: for, you see, it is already in snuff.

HIPPOLYTA I am aweary of this moon: would he would change!

THESEUS It appears, by his small light of discretion, that he is in the wane: but yet, in courtesy, in all reason, we must stay the time.

LYSANDER Proceed, moon.

MOON All that I have to say, is to tell you that the lantern is the moon; I, the man i' the moon; this thorn-bush, my thorn-bush; and this dog, my dog.

DEMETRIUS Why, all these should be in the lantern; for all these are in the moon. But silence; here comes Thisbe.

[Enter THISBE.]

THISBE This is old Ninny's tomb. Where is my love?

LION Oh!

[The LION roars.--THISBE runs off.]

DEMETRIUS Well roared, lion.

THESEUS Well run, Thisbe.

HIPPOLYTA Well shone, moon.--Truly, the moon shines with a good grace.

[The LION tears THISBE'S Mantle, and exit.]

THESEUS Well moused, lion.

DEMETRIUS And so comes Pyramus.

LYSANDER And then the lion vanishes.

[Enter PYRAMUS.]

PYRAMUS Sweet moon, I thank thee for thy sunny beams; I thank thee, moon, for shining now so bright: For, by thy gracious golden, glittering streams, I trust to take of truest Thisby's sight. But stay;--O spite! But mark,--poor knight, What dreadful dole is here! Eyes, do you see? How can it be? O dainty duck! O dear! Thy mantle good, What! stained with blood? Approach, ye furies fell! O fates! come, come; Cut thread and thrum; Quail, rush, conclude, and quell!

THESEUS This passion, and the death of a dear friend, would go near to make a man look sad.

HIPPOLYTA Beshrew my heart, but I pity the man.

PYRAMUS O wherefore, nature, didst thou lions frame? Since lion vile hath here deflower'd my dear; Which is--no, no-- which was the fairest dame That liv'd, that lov'd, that lik'd, that look'd with cheer. Come, tears, confound; Out, sword, and wound The pap of Pyramus: Ay, that left pap, Where heart doth hop:-- Thus die I, thus, thus, thus. Now am I dead, Now am I fled; My soul is in the sky: Tongue, lose thy light! Moon, take thy flight! Now die, die, die, die, die.

[Dies. Exit MOONSHINE.]

DEMETRIUS No die, but an ace, for him; for he is but one.

LYSANDER Less than an ace, man; for he is dead; he is nothing.

THESEUS With the help of a surgeon he might yet recover and prove an ass.

HIPPOLYTA How chance moonshine is gone before Thisbe comes back and finds her lover?

THESEUS She will find him by starlight.--Here she comes; and her passion ends the play.

[Enter THISBE.]

HIPPOLYTA Methinks she should not use a long one for such a Pyramus: I hope she will be brief.

DEMETRIUS A mote will turn the balance, which Pyramus, which Thisbe, is the better.

LYSANDER She hath spied him already with those sweet eyes.

DEMETRIUS And thus she moans, videlicet.--

THISBE Asleep, my love? What, dead, my dove? O Pyramus, arise, Speak, speak. Quite dumb? Dead, dead? A tomb Must cover thy sweet eyes. These lily lips, This cherry nose, These yellow cowslip cheeks, Are gone, are gone: Lovers, make moan! His eyes were green as leeks. O Sisters Three, Come, come to me, With hands as pale as milk; Lay them in gore, Since you have shore With shears his thread of silk. Tongue, not a word:-- Come, trusty sword; Come, blade, my breast imbrue; And farewell, friends:-- Thus Thisbe ends; Adieu, adieu, adieu.

[Dies.]

THESEUS Moonshine and lion are left to bury the dead.

DEMETRIUS Ay, and wall too.

BOTTOM No, I assure you; the wall is down that parted their fathers. Will it please you to see the epilogue, or to hear a Bergomask dance between two of our company?

THESEUS No epilogue, I pray you; for your play needs no excuse. Never excuse; for when the players are all dead there need none to be blamed. Marry, if he that writ it had played Pyramus, and hang'd himself in Thisbe's garter, it would have been a fine tragedy: and so it is, truly; and very notably discharged. But come, your Bergomask; let your epilogue alone.

[Here a dance of Clowns.]

The iron tongue of midnight hath told twelve:-- Lovers, to bed; 'tis almost fairy time. I fear we shall out-sleep the coming morn, As much as we this night have overwatch'd. This palpable-gross play hath well beguil'd The heavy gait of night.--Sweet friends, to bed.-- A fortnight hold we this solemnity, In nightly revels and new jollity.

[Exeunt.]

Scene II

[Enter PUCK.]

PUCK Now the hungry lion roars, And the wolf behowls the moon; Whilst the heavy ploughman snores, All with weary task fordone. Now the wasted brands do glow, Whilst the scritch-owl, scritching loud, Puts the wretch that lies in woe In remembrance of a shroud. Now it is the time of night That the graves, all gaping wide, Every one lets forth its sprite, In the church-way paths to glide: And we fairies, that do run By the triple Hecate's team From the presence of the sun, Following darkness like a dream, Now are frolic; not a mouse Shall disturb this hallow'd house: I am sent with broom before, To sweep the dust behind the door.

[Enter OBERON and TITANIA, with their Train.]

OBERON Through the house give glimmering light, By the dead and drowsy fire: Every elf and fairy sprite Hop as light as bird from brier: And this ditty, after me, Sing and dance it trippingly.

TITANIA First, rehearse your song by rote, To each word a warbling note; Hand in hand, with fairy grace, Will we sing, and bless this place.

[Song and Dance.]

OBERON Now, until the break of day, Through this house each fairy stray, To the best bride-bed will we, Which by us shall blessed be; And the issue there create Ever shall be fortunate. So shall all the couples three Ever true in loving be; And the blots of Nature's hand Shall not in their issue stand: Never mole, hare-lip, nor scar, Nor mark prodigious, such as are Despised in nativity, Shall upon their children be.-- With this field-dew consecrate, Every fairy take his gate; And each several chamber bless, Through this palace, with sweet peace; E'er shall it in safety rest, And the owner of it blest. Trip away: Make no stay: Meet me all by break of day.

[Exeunt OBERON, TITANIA, and Train.]

PUCK If we shadows have offended, Think but this,--and all is mended,-- That you have but slumber'd here While these visions did appear. And this weak and idle theme, No more yielding but a dream, Gentles, do not reprehend; If you pardon, we will mend. And, as I am an honest Puck, If we have unearned luck Now to 'scape the serpent's tongue, We will make amends ere long; Else the Puck a liar call: So, good night unto you all. Give me your hands, if we be friends, And Robin shall restore amends.

[Exit.]

About BookCaps

We all need refreshers every now and then. Whether you are a student trying to cram for that big final, or someone just trying to understand a book more, BookCaps can help. We are a small, but growing company, and are adding titles every month.

Visit www.bookcaps.com to see more of our books, or contact us with any questions.

Made in the USA
Lexington, KY
12 August 2014